BACKPACKER

The Magazine Of Wilderness Travel

Wilderness
911

A STEP-BY-STEP
GUIDE FOR
MEDICAL
EMERGENCIES
AND IMPROVISED
CARE IN THE
BACKCOUNTRY

THE MOUNTAINEERS BOOKS

Published by
The Mountaineers
1001 SW Klickitat Way, Suite 201
Seattle, WA 98134

BACKPACKER
The Magazine Of Wilderness Travel
33 East Minor Street
Emmaus, PA 18098

First printing 1998, second printing 2001, third printing 2003

Published simultaneously in Great Britain by Cordee, 3a DeMontfort Street, Leicester, England, LE1 7HD

Manufactured in the United States of America

Edited by Mary Anne Stewart
Illustrations by Dawn Peterson
Cover design by Jennifer Shontz
Book design and layout by Ani Rucki

Library of Congress Cataloging-in-Publication Data
Weiss, Eric A., M.D.
    Wilderness 911 : a step-by-step guide for medical emergencies and
improvised care in the backcountry / by Eric A. Weiss.—1st ed.
        p.   cm.
    Includes index.
    ISBN 0-89886-597-2
    1. Outdoor medical emergencies. I. Title.
    RC88.9.O95W45   1998
    616.02'5—dc21   98-39861
                                                     CIP

This book is dedicated to my parents, Gerald and Libby,

for unselfishly devoting their lives to the health and happiness

of their children and grandchildren, and to my wife, Amy,

for her unshakable love, companionship, and care,

and for helping me to better balance my life.

Contents

Acknowledgments

I WOULD LIKE TO ACKNOWLEDGE, and express my sincere appreciation to, all of the friends and colleagues who have helped to develop and grow the field of wilderness medicine. Their experience, expertise, wisdom, and devotion to the field are reflected in many parts of the book. In particular I would like to acknowledge Paul Auerbach, M.D., Howard Donner, M.D., Peter Hackett, M.D., Findlay Russell, M.D., Robert Norris, M.D., Joe Serra, M.D., Lanny Johnson, M.D., David Schlim, M.D., Howard Backer, M.D., Gary Kibbee, Warren Berg, Stephen Lyons, Henry Herrmann, D.D.S., Mel Otten, M.D., Ken Zafren, M.D., Brownie Shoene, M.D., Jim Bagian, M.D., Barbara Kennedy, M.D., Doug Gentile, M.D., Daniel Danzl, M.D., Elaine Jong, M.D., and Frank Hubbel, D.O.

Thanks are also owed to Mary Anne Stewart for her careful editing, to Uma Kukathas and Margaret Foster of The Mountaineers Books and John Viehman of *Backpacker* Magazine for their support, and to Dawn Peterson for her wonderful illustrations.

I would also like to extend special thanks to Kate Nevin for all of her admininstrative assistance and support and to acknowledge and thank Sam Anagnostou, Frank Costco, Captain John Cadell, Stacey Hansen, Robert Norris, M.D., and Dolly Kagawa for their unwavering friendship and support.

Introduction

IMAGINE YOURSELF IN THE MIDDLE OF the wilderness, kneeling beside a fallen hiker who has suffered multiple injuries. If you were at your job or at home, you could call 911 and then provide first-aid care until the paramedics arrived. In the backcountry you may have to rely on yourself and your party for several hours, or even days, before professional medical care can be obtained. *Wilderness 911* was written to help you manage emergencies and illnesses when you can't call 911.

The book is a step-by-step guide to performing first aid and more advanced medical care in remote areas when professional help is at least one hour away and medical supplies are limited or absent. It covers common emergencies that are unique to the backcountry. In most situations, the treatment recommendations go beyond first aid and explain how to diagnose and manage a problem in a more comprehensive manner.

Wilderness 911 also emphasizes improvised techniques for treating specific injuries and illnesses. It offers creative solutions for fabricating bandages, splints, and even medication from whatever is at hand.

This book is not a substitute for taking a comprehensive first-aid or wilderness medicine course, or for seeking prompt medical care in the event of an illness or accident. Taking a course in wilderness first aid—and practicing your skills before you leave home—will better prepare you to manage an emergency when it occurs. Keep in mind that you should not attempt to perform any procedure you're uncomfortable with, unless the victim will die or suffer serious consequences without your intervention. And remember that in all serious situations your first priority after administering appropriate first aid should be to obtain professional medical attention as soon as possible.

Before leaving on a backcountry trip, consult your physician concerning any medications that you intend to carry with you. Inquire about potential complications or side effects and make sure you are not allergic to any drugs you intend to use. Be aware that sharing medications with others is potentially dangerous and is not recommended.

HOW TO USE THIS BOOK

After working in a busy emergency department for more than ten years, I can honestly say that I only use about 10 percent of the information learned during my four years of medical school. Ninety percent of what I was taught has nothing to do with taking care of patients in an emergency setting and has long since been forgotten.

This same "10 percent" rule holds true for wilderness medicine. When you get past the fluff and look at what's really important in rendering medical care in the backcountry, only about 10 percent of what you generally read actually matters. In *Wilderness 911,* I have tried to highlight this key information and present it in a step-by-step manner that facilitates the art of diagnosis and treatment.

Quick diagnosis and treatment are the essence of both emergency and wilderness medicine. An ER doc usually has only a few minutes to figure out what's wrong with a patient and come up with a game plan before being called to see another patient. The goal is to keep it simple, focus on the major problems, and quickly render definitive treatment. Your goal in providing effective wilderness medical care is the same.

Wilderness 911 is organized into two parts. Part I provides a general overview of what to expect and how to respond in the event of a medical emergency. The basic life-saving emergency techniques are discussed and explained. You should read through Part I carefully and make sure you understand the basic concepts and techniques thoroughly before going out on a backcountry trip—they are the foundation for your emergency response in any situation.

Part II covers specific conditions and gives simple directions for how to treat them. This part of the book is organized into chapters according to related injuries and illnesses—Head Injuries, Abdominal Injuries, Fractures, Burns, and so forth. Following a general introduction to the conditions covered, the various chapters address prevention, specific conditions, signs and symptoms, and treatment. "When to Worry" sections call attention to situations in which immediate evacuation is required and "Backcountry Tricks" sidebars highlight possible improvisations.

Prevention. Prevention of illness or injury is the first and most important step in backcountry medicine. You can avoid many medical problems by better understanding the environment and by taking certain precautions. Each chapter describes such precautions whenever they can be taken.

Signs and Symptoms. Diagnosis of an injury or illness relies on the ability of the rescuer to examine the victim thoroughly and identify important medical clues called signs and symptoms. *Signs* are the things you observe when you examine a victim with your eyes, ears, nose, and hands—for example, you might see bluish discoloration of the skin, hear labored or noisy breathing, smell pus in a wound infection, or feel swelling under the skin. *Symptoms* are what the victim tells you he is experiencing, such as pain, nausea, dizziness, or a headache.

Each chapter is broken down into specific illnesses and injuries, each of which has a list of signs and symptoms that will help you diagnose that particular condition. *Please note that for each condition, either some or all of the signs and symptoms described may be present.* You should look for these clues in the victim in order to administer the most appropriate treatment plan.

Treatment. For each illness or injury, a treatment section outlines an appropriate treatment plan for that condition.

Note that there may be more than one correct way to treat a particular problem, and the rescuer and victim should both be comfortable with the treatment decision. You should always weigh the relative benefit of any procedure or treatment you intend to administer against its potential risks and complications. Ultimately, the most appropriate treatment for a particular problem will depend on many variables, including your own resources, training, experience, the distance from civilization, and whether or not the situation is desperate.

When to Worry. The "When to Worry," sections (marked with a 💣) will help you identify situations in which immediate evacuation from the wilderness is recommended. When in doubt, it is always better to get out and seek help rather than wait and see what happens. For more information on emergency evacuation, see Appendix C.

The 💣 symbol is also used to identify individual conditions that are serious enough to warrant evacuation or a visit to a medical facility as soon as possible.

Backcountry Tricks. The "Backcountry Tricks" sidebars describe tricks and techniques for improvising medical supplies and care from simple materials on hand. Improvisation is at the heart of wilderness medicine and is limited only by your imagination and creativity. These sections are marked with a 💡

Warning: This book does not give you license to practice medicine in the wilderness. It is always better to err on the side of caution, and to be more conservative when the condition is not life threatening, than try to do something that you are not trained to do. If the victim is conscious, you should advise him of your level of training and experience and, when possible, obtain written approval from him before performing any procedure that may have associated complications or risks.

PART I

WHAT TO DO FIRST
IN AN EMERGENCY

CHAPTER I

Life-Saving Techniques: The Three ABC's

WHEN YOU FIRST ENCOUNTER THE scene of an accident in the backcountry, you may feel fear, panic, or hopelessness, and your heart rate and breathing may soar. These reactions are normal—you should expect and accept that you will feel a great deal of anxiety in an emergency situation. Probably the most effective means to overcome this inevitable anxiety response is to *prepare yourself before you go into the wilderness* by acquiring the skills (and thus the confidence) needed to tackle medical emergencies. This chapter discusses the first, most important actions you need to perform when you encounter an ill or injured person in the backcountry. These first steps are what is known in emergency medicine as "the primary survey."

You need to learn the contents of this chapter thoroughly before going out into the wilderness. If someone has stopped breathing, you must be ready to act instantly—you don't have time to start reading a book. Practicing these skills before you leave home—especially by taking a course in CPR or first aid—will better prepare you to manage a life-threatening emergency when it occurs.

DESIGNATE A LEADER

In a group situation, developing a team approach at the site of the accident is vital to the success of the rescue. Begin by designating a leader. This individual can be the climb leader, the head boatman, or anyone else who assumes the role. This person should direct all first-aid efforts and, when possible, should delegate duties, rather than perform them. If the leader becomes intimately involved in a specific function, he or she loses the ability to maintain a team effort. The leader should evaluate the victim's injuries, the party size, and the terrain, and develop a plan for either evacuating the victim or obtaining professional assistance.

THE THREE ABC'S

The acronym ABC (airway-breathing-circulation) is often used in urban medicine to help a rescuer remember the three life-saving priorities in the primary survey of a victim. For wilderness rescue, I've expanded the acronym to the "three ABC's" (three A's, three B's, and three C's) because of the additional challenges of the wilderness environment.

When you are confronted with a sick or injured person in the backcountry, *the first thing to do is follow the three ABC's.* They are the nine initial priorities in wilderness first aid. Perform them in order (first all the A's, then all the B's, then all the C's) to assess the scene and victim, determine what life-threatening condition may need your attention, and begin treatment.

The Three ABC's

A1. Assess the scene
A2. Airway (ensure an open airway)
A3. Alert others

B1. Barriers (gloves, mask)
B2. Breathing (check for breathing and perform rescue breathing if necessary)
B3. Bleeding (stop bleeding)

C1. Circulation (start CPR if the victim has no pulse)
C2. Cervical spine (prevent unnecessary movement of the head and neck)
C3. Cover and protect the victim from the environment

A1. Assess the Scene

Assess the scene for further hazards to yourself or to the victim—such as rockfall, avalanche, and dangerous animals—before rendering any first-aid care. Always ensure the safety of the noninjured members of the party first. The worst thing you can do is create another victim or become one yourself. Avoid approaching the victim from directly above if there is a possibility of a rock or snow slide. Do not allow your sense of urgency to transform an accident into a risky and foolish rescue attempt.

A2. Airway

Make sure the victim is breathing and does not have an obstructed airway. Speak loudly to the victim as you approach—a response indicates that he is breathing and has a pulse. With infants and children, gently tap them on the hands and feet and call their name.

If the victim is unresponsive, immediately determine if he is breathing. If he is face down, logroll him onto his back so that the head, shoulders, and torso move as a single unit without twisting (fig. 1A–B). Place your ear and cheek close to the victim's mouth and nose to detect air movement. At the same time, look for movement of the chest and stomach (fig. 2). In cold weather, look for a vapor cloud and feel for warm air movement.

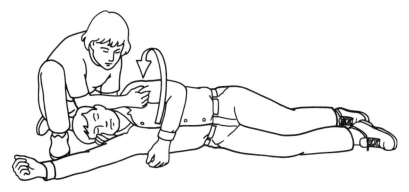

Figure 1A. One rescuer logrolling victim onto his back so that the head, shoulders, and torso move as a single unit.

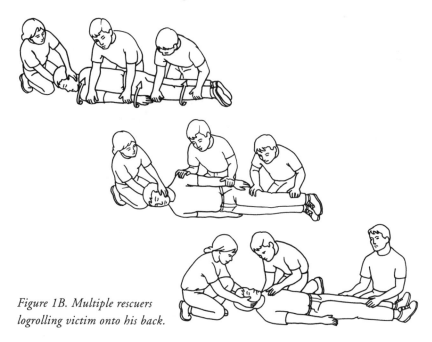

Figure 1B. Multiple rescuers logrolling victim onto his back.

If no movement of air is detected, clean the victim's mouth out with your fingers and open the airway. If you do not suspect a neck injury, you can open the airway by placing the palm of one hand on the victim's forehead and tilt his head back while you grasp and lift his chin with the fingers of your other hand (fig. 3). Monitor for air movement as above.

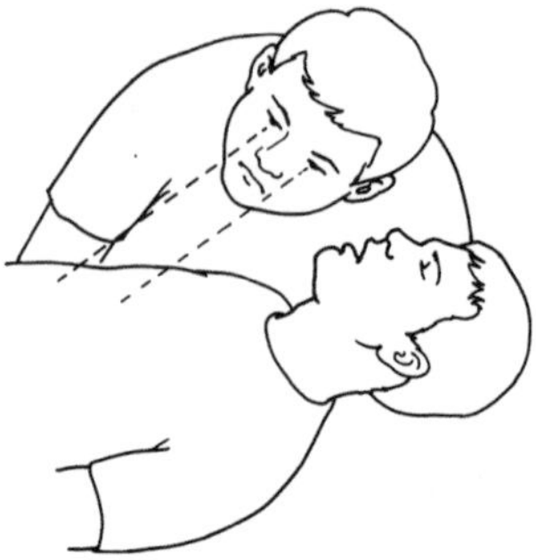

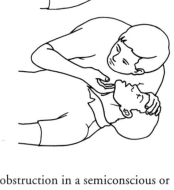

Figure 2. Is the victim breathing? Place your ear and cheek close to the unconscious victim's mouth and nose to detect air movement. Look for movement of the chest and stomach.

Figure 3. "Open" the airway in an unconscious victim who is not breathing (if you do not suspect a neck injury) by tilting his head back while you grasp and lift his chin. Look for movement at the chest and stomach to signify breathing.

The most common reason for an airway obstruction in a semiconscious or unconscious victim is that the muscles of the tongue and throat relax, allowing the tongue to fall back and block the airway. If the victim is unconscious after trauma, use the jaw-thrust technique to open the airway (this technique minimizes movement of the neck): kneel down with your knees on either side of the victim's head, place your hands on either side of the victim's jawbone, and push the base of the jaw upward (fig. 4).

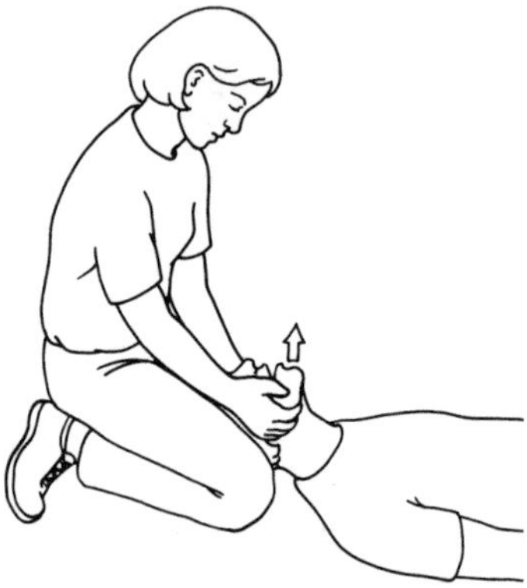

Figure 4. Jaw thrust technique for opening the airway in a semiconscious or unconscious victim after trauma when a spine injury may be present. The jaw thrust minimizes movement of the neck.

Clearing the Airway in a Choking Victim

Choking is a life-threatening emergency that occurs when a foreign object obstructs the victim's airway so that he cannot breathe. Choking should be suspected when an individual suddenly becomes agitated and clutches his throat, especially while eating. The victim may be unable to speak and then become cyanotic (turn blue).

The Heimlich Maneuver

The Heimlich maneuver, also called abdominal thrusts, is a maneuver which pushes the diaphragm quickly upward, forcing enough air from the lungs to dislodge and dispel the foreign object. The same maneuver may be used on both adults and children.

1. Stand behind the victim and wrap your arms around the victim's waist (fig. 5A). Make a fist with one of your hands and place it just above the victim's navel and below the rib cage, with the thumb side against his abdomen (fig. 5B).
2. Grasp your fist with your other hand and pull it forcefully toward you, into the victim's abdomen and slightly upward, with a quick thrust. If unsuccessful, the procedure should be repeated.

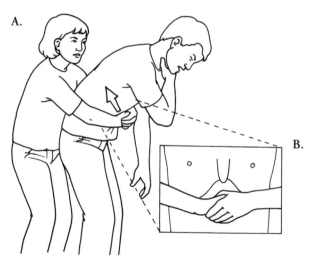

Figure 5A–B. Heimlich maneuver: standing.

If the victim becomes unconscious:
1. Lay the victim on his back and attempt rescue breathing (see p. 22).
2. If you cannot get air into the victim and/or the chest does not rise with rescue breathing, perform the Heimlich maneuver while kneeling down and straddling the victim's thighs (fig. 6). Use the heel of your hand instead of your fist.

3. If the maneuver is still unsuccessful, sweep the mouth with one or two fingers to try to remove any foreign material. Continue to perform the Heimlich maneuver and periodically attempt rescue breathing.

Figure 6. Heimlich maneuver: lying down.

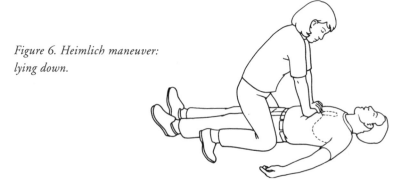

🔆 Backcountry Tricks
Keeping the Airway Open in an Unconscious Victim

Keeping the airway open with the jaw-thrust technique ties up your hands. If you are by yourself, you can keep a victim's airway open by pinning the front of the victim's tongue to his lower lip with two safety pins. As an alternative to pinning the tongue to the lower lip, you can pass a string or shoelace through the pins in the tongue and keep the tongue forward by tying it to the victim's shirt button or jacket zipper.

This technique sounds barbaric, but it effectively pulls the tongue forward and prevents it from obstructing the airway. It also frees up your hands for other tasks. Any victim who requires this life-saving maneuver will probably not mind the small holes and will, of course, not notice the discomfort.

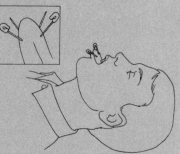

Figure 7. Pinning the front of an unconscious victim's tongue to his lower lip with two safety pins to open his airway.

A3. Alert Others

Take a few seconds to call or send someone for help. Or alert others to the accident by yelling or blowing a whistle before further tending to the victim's needs. Taking a few seconds early on to get reinforcements can make a big difference down the road.

B1. Barriers

Anytime you deal with blood or bodily fluids, it's vitally important to protect yourself from blood-borne pathogens such as hepatitis and the AIDS virus. One out of every three hundred persons in the United States is now infected with the HIV virus, and the risk of infectious hepatitis is even greater.

Protect your hands with virus-proof gloves, and use a barrier device when performing mouth-to-mouth rescue breathing (see figs. 8 and 9). Don't use vinyl gloves because studies show they leak too often. Even latex gloves can leak, so be sure to wash your hands, or to wipe them with an antiseptic towelette, after removing the gloves. Dispose of bloody gloves by securing them in a waterproof bag.

Warning: Around 5 to 7 percent of the population, and more than 8 percent of all medical personnel, are allergic to latex. Latex allergies can produce skin rashes, severe anaphylactic reactions (see p. 36), and death. If you suspect that you may have an allergy to latex, carry nitrile gloves in your first-aid kit.

If you don't have latex or nitrile gloves you can improvise.

 Backcountry Tricks
Improvising Barrier Gloves

Any gloves are better than using your bare hands. Dishwashing gloves make an effective barrier to blood. An improvised glove can be made by placing your hand inside a sandwich or garbage bag and securing it to your wrist with tape or string.

◌ Backcountry Tricks
Improvising a CPR Barrier

You can modify a latex or other nitrile glove to make a barrier shield for performing rescue breathing. Simply make a slit in the middle finger of the glove at its halfway point (A) and insert it into the victim's mouth (B). Stretch the glove across the victim's mouth and nose (C) and blow into the glove as you would to inflate a balloon. After each breath remove the part of the glove covering the nose to allow the victim to exhale (D). The slit creates a one-way valve, preventing backflow of the victim's saliva.

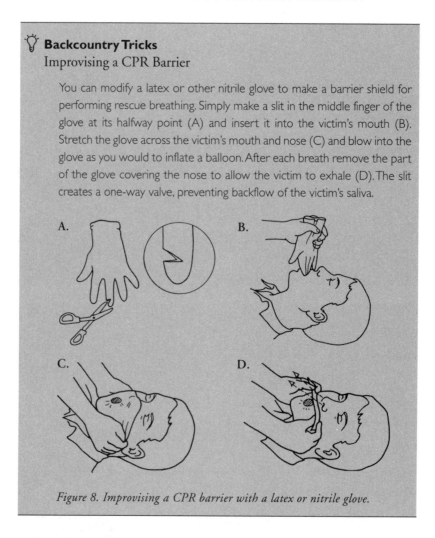

Figure 8. Improvising a CPR barrier with a latex or nitrile glove.

B2. Breathing

If the victim does not breathe on his own after you have established an airway, begin mouth-to-mouth rescue breathing.

Rescue Breathing: Adults

1. Pinch the victim's nostrils closed and place your mouth over his mouth. Use a CPR barrier or a modified glove (see above) to prevent physical contact with the victim's mouth (fig. 9A).
2. Blow air into the victim until you see the chest rise. Remove your mouth to allow the victim to exhale. Give two initial breaths (fig. 9B).

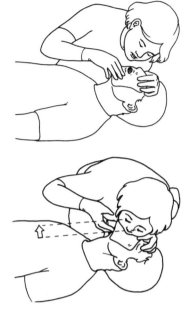

Figure 9A. Applying a CPR microshield one-way barrier device to the victim prior to performing mouth-to-mouth rescue breathing.

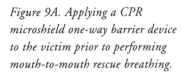

Figure 9B. Rescue breathing using a barrier device.

3. Repeat this procedure, giving a vigorous breath every 5 seconds until the victim starts to breathe spontaneously, help arrives, or you are too exhausted to continue.

4. If air does not move in and out of the victim's mouth easily or you do not detect chest movement, first try tilting the head farther back, or, if you suspect a cervical spine injury, repeat the jaw-thrust technique, pushing the victim's jaw farther out. If the victim still does not start breathing, the airway may be obstructed by a foreign body, and you will need to clear it (see above).

5. During mouth-to-mouth rescue breathing, the victim's stomach often may fill with air, eventually resulting in vomiting. If vomiting occurs, logroll the victim in a manner that maintains alignment of the cervical spine (see fig.1), and clear the airway by sweeping two fingers through the victim's mouth.

6. Check for a pulse by feeling for the carotid artery in the victim's neck (see p. 26). If the victim is hypothermic (see p. 164), feel for 1 full minute before deciding that he has no pulse. If a pulse is present, continue rescue breathing. If no pulse is present, start chest compressions (see below).

Rescue Breathing: Children

1. Cover the child's mouth with your mouth. Pinch the child's nose closed with the thumb and forefinger of your hand, using the hand you have placed on the forehead for the head tilt. Use your other hand to lift the chin.

2. Breathe two slow (1- to 1½-second) breaths into the child's mouth, with a 2-second pause in between breaths. You should breathe enough air in to allow the child's chest to rise.

3. If the child does not start to breathe on his own, check for a pulse. If a pulse is present, continue rescue breathing with 20 breaths per minute. If no pulse is present, start chest compressions (see p. 28).

B3. Bleeding

Carefully check the victim for signs of profuse bleeding. With a gloved hand, feel inside any bulky clothing and check underneath the victim for signs of bleeding. To stop bleeding, use your gloved hand to apply pressure directly to the wound (fig. 10). Use whatever clean material is available, and then, as time allows, replace it with sterile gauze (from your first-aid kit) to hold pressure. The idea is not to soak up blood with a big wad of bandage material, but to apply focused and firm pressure directly on the bleeding site.

Many first-aid manuals still recommend the use of "pressure points" to help stop bleeding. This technique, of applying pressure to a large artery above (upstream from) the bleeding site has minimal benefit since almost all areas of the body are supplied by more than one artery. Pressure points can be used as an adjunct to, but should never be a substitute for, direct pressure on the wound itself.

In almost all cases, the pressure will stop the bleeding. It may be necessary to hold pressure for up to 30 minutes. If you need to free up your hands, create a pressure dressing by wrapping an elastic bandage tightly around a stack of 4 by 4 inch sterile gauze pads placed over the wound.

If bleeding from an extremity cannot be stopped by direct pressure, and the victim is in danger of bleeding to death, apply a tourniquet (see below). A tourniquet is any band applied around an extremity so tightly that all blood flow beyond the band is cut off. If the tourniquet is left on for more than 2 hours, the arm or leg beyond the tourniquet may die and require amputation.

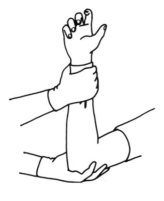

Figure 10. To stop bleeding, use your gloved hand to apply pressure directly to the wound.

💡 Backcountry Tricks
Applying a Tourniquet

1. Tourniquet material should be wide and flat, to prevent crushing body tissue. Use a firm bandage, belt, or strap that is 3 to 4 inches wide and that will not stretch. Never use wire, rope, or any material that will cut the skin (A).
2. Wrap the bandage snugly around the extremity as close above the wound as possible and tie an overhand knot (B).
3. Place a stick or similar object on the knot and tie another overhand knot over the stick (C).
4. Twist the stick until the bandage becomes tight enough to stop the bleeding. Tie or tape the stick in place to prevent it from unraveling (D).
5. Write "TK" and the time the tourniquet was applied on the victim (the forehead is a good location) to keep track of how long the tourniquet is in place.

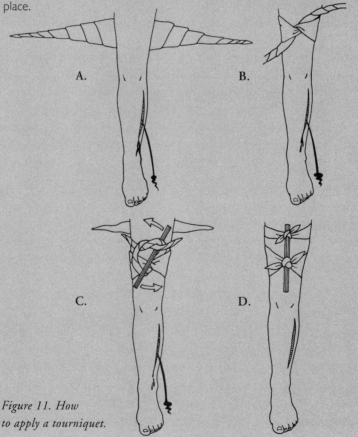

Figure 11. How to apply a tourniquet.

6. If you are more than 1 hour from medical care, loosen the tourniquet very slowly at the end of 1 hour while maintaining direct pressure on the wound. If bleeding is again heavy, retighten the tourniquet. If bleeding is now manageable with direct pressure alone, leave the tourniquet in place, but do not tighten it again unless severe bleeding starts.

Warning:

1. **Do not leave a tourniquet on for over 2 hours, because tissue beyond the tourniquet will die and the extremity may require amputation.**
2. **Never apply direct pressure to a bleeding neck wound, because it can interfere with breathing. Instead, carefully pinch the wound closed.**
3. **Never apply direct pressure to the eye, because you could cause permanent damage.**

C1.   Circulation

Check to see if the victim has a pulse (heartbeat). Place your index and middle fingers on the victim's throat over the Adam's apple, then slide your fingers down the side of the victim's neck toward the ground to the space between the Adam's apple and neck muscle to find the carotid pulse (fig. 12).

Hold your fingers over the carotid artery for at least 30 seconds—or 60 seconds if the victim is hypothermic (see p. 164)—and feel for any pulsations. If you do not detect a pulse, begin cardiopulmonary resuscitation (CPR), combining chest compressions (see below) with mouth-to-mouth rescue breathing (see above).

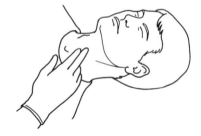

Figure 12. Feeling the carotid pulse in the neck.

When to Start and Stop CPR

Do not be afraid to start CPR, fearing that you might be criticized for not continuing it indefinitely. There is an old saying in medicine that "once started, CPR should never be stopped in the field." Not only is this dictum archaic, it is also wrong and potentially hazardous to rescuers, who might put themselves at risk attempting to continue CPR in a dangerous situation. It is well established that after 10 to 15 minutes of CPR, if the victim does not respond with a return of spontaneous heartbeat and breathing, he never will. The only *rare* exceptions are victims who are profoundly hypothermic.

I recommend giving the victim the benefit of the doubt and starting CPR even if he has been without a heartbeat or breath for a prolonged time. It is difficult to know exactly how long a person found unconscious has actually been in cardiac arrest. If you are not successful in resuscitating the victim after 15 to 30 minutes of CPR, and the victim is not profoundly hypothermic, you can discontinue the effort. You will know that you have given it your best shot. If the victim is profoundly hypothermic, continue CPR until he reaches a medical facility or it is dangerous or you are too exhausted to continue.

Chest Compressions: Adults

1. Place the victim on his back on a firm surface. Position the heel of one hand over the center of the victim's breastbone, two fingers up from the xyphoid (fig. 13A), and the heel of your second hand over the bottom hand, interlocking the fingers (fig. 13B).
2. Your shoulders should line up directly over the victim's breastbone when your elbows are held straight (fig. 13C).

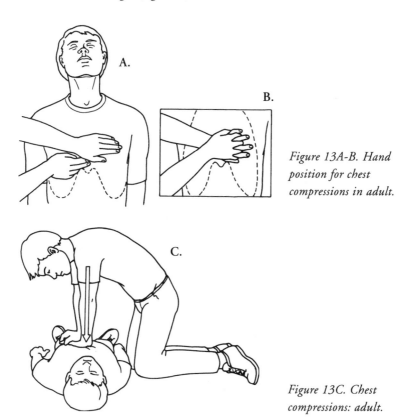

Figure 13A-B. Hand position for chest compressions in adult.

Figure 13C. Chest compressions: adult.

3. Keeping your arms stiff, compress the breastbone 1½ to 2 inches and then release. Use a smooth motion for both the compression and the release. The compression phase should equal the relaxation phase, with a rate of 80 to100 compressions per minute (count out loud, "one-and-two-and-three-and . . . ", giving a compression for each number). Do not remove your hands from the victim's chest between compressions.

4. If two rescuers are working together, the first rescuer should pause after every fifth compression so the second rescuer can give the victim a mouth-to-mouth breath. If a single person is performing the rescue, he should alternate ten chest compressions with two breaths. During CPR, the rescuer should check every few minutes for return of a carotid pulse or spontaneous breathing.

Chest Compressions: Children (older than 1 year)

1. Place the heel of your hand on the child's lower breastbone, with your fingers lifted off the chest (fig. 14).

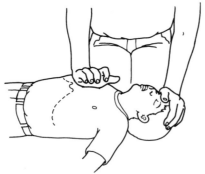

Figure 14. Chest compressions: child.

2. Compress the breastbone about one-third to one-half the thickness of the chest (1 to 1½ inches).

3. Compress the chest approximately 100 times per minute, stopping to give the child a breath every five compressions.

4. Continue the compression-to-breathing ratio of five to one. Use this same ratio whether one or two persons are doing the resuscitation. Stop to check for spontaneous breathing and a pulse after 1 minute, and then after every few minutes.

C2. Cervical Spine

The spinal cord, which runs down through the vertebrae in the neck and back, is vital for life. If the spinal cord is damaged, the victim can suffer permanent paralysis or death. If you suspect an injury to the cervical spine (the neck vertebrae), immobilize the victim's head, neck, and torso to prevent any movement of the head in relation to the body (see below). Avoid moving a victim with a suspected spine injury if he is in a safe location. The victim should be evacuated by professional rescuers (see Appendix C). 🐾

You should suspect a spine injury if the victim has suffered a traumatic accident such as a fall, a head injury, or a diving injury, and if any of the following signs or symptoms are present:

- The victim is unconscious.
- The victim complains of neck or back pain.
- The back of the neck or the backbone is tender when touched.
- There is numbness, tingling, or altered sensation in the extremities (arms, legs, hands, or feet).
- The victim is unable to move or has weakness in an arm or leg that is not caused by direct trauma to that part.
- The victim has an altered level of consciousness or is under the influence of drugs or alcohol.
- The victim has another very painful injury that may distract him from the pain in his neck, such as a fracture of the femur (thigh bone), a dislocated shoulder, or a broken rib.

💡 Backcountry Tricks
Stabilizing the Cervical Spine

Placing your knees on either side of the victim's head, and holding his head securely between your thighs, effectively stabilizes the victim's cervical spine without tying up your hands.

C3. Cover and Protect the Victim

If it is cold, place insulating materials, garments, blankets or a sleeping pad, underneath and on top of the victim to protect him from hypothermia. Remove and replace any wet clothing. If it is hot, loosen the victim's clothing and create shade. If the victim is in a dangerous area, move him to a safer location while maintaining spine immobilization if indicated.

AFTER THE THREE ABC'S

Once you have completed the primary survey and made sure that there are no life-threatening problems, perform a head-to-toe examination of the victim, looking for further evidence of injury. Look for signs and symptoms of illness or injury. Gently push on every part of the victim, looking for swelling, pain, or deformity.

Take note of what you discover and then refer to the chapters in Part II to assist you in diagnosing and treating the problem.

TREATMENT OF SPECIFIC ILLNESSES AND INJURIES

CHAPTER 2

Shock

SHOCK IS A LIFE-THREATENING CONDITION in which blood flow to the tissues or vital organs of the body is inadequate and cells are therefore deprived of oxygen, which is carried by the blood. In 1852, shock was defined as "a rude unhinging of the machinery of life." Probably no better definition exists to describe the devastating effects that shock can have, especially in the wilderness, where it is difficult to treat.

Any serious injury or illness can produce shock, especially severe bleeding (either external or internal), fractures of the femur (thigh bone) or pelvis, major burns, dehydration, heart failure, severe allergic reactions, or spinal cord injuries with paralysis. However, you should look for signs of shock in any victim who is injured or ill. Although there is little that a layperson can do to treat shock in the wilderness, it is vital that you be able to recognize it, because it means that the victim is in serious trouble and needs immediate evacuation to a medical facility (see Appendix C). 💣⃰

TYPES OF SHOCK

It is important to understand and recognize the different causes of shock, since its treatment in the backcountry can differ depending upon the type.

Hypovolemic shock. The word *hypovolemic* means, literally, "not enough volume of blood." In hypovolemic shock, there is not enough blood or body fluids to provide adequate circulation to all parts of the body. There are two types of hypovolemic shock:

1. *External hypovolemic shock,* caused by external loss of fluids that you can see, such as in:
- Bleeding from a wound.
- Dehydration from profuse diarrhea, vomiting, or sweating.
2. *Internal hypovolemic shock,* caused by internal loss of fluids into body cavities that you can't see, such as in:
- Bleeding from a ruptured or lacerated organ, such as the spleen or liver.
- Bleeding from a fractured pelvis or femur.

Cardiogenic shock (heart failure). In cardiogenic ("originating in the heart") shock, the heart is weakened, usually as the result of a heart attack, and fails to pump enough blood to the rest of the body.

Vasogenic shock. In vasogenic ("originating in the vessels") shock, the blood vessels dilate, causing blood to pool in the veins. There is insufficient blood returning to the heart, and thus not enough blood is circulated to the vital organs. There are four types of vasogenic shock:

1. *Spinal shock.* Spinal shock is caused by injury to the spinal cord. The injury produces paralysis and the nervous system loses control over the blood vessels and they dilate. The heart rate does not speed up as it would in other types of shock despite low blood pressure.

2. *Anaphylactic shock.* Anaphylactic ("hyperallergic," or hypersensitive) shock is a severe allergic reaction that causes the blood vessels to dilate.

3. *Psychogenic shock.* In psychogenic ("originating in the mind") shock, the victim experiences something unpleasant that causes the heart rate to slow down, the blood vessels to dilate, and the blood pressure to drop. The result is that the victim faints.

4. *Septic shock.* Toxins (poisonous substances) from a severe infection make the blood vessels dilate, which lowers blood pressure.

💣 External Hypovolemic Shock

SIGNS AND SYMPTOMS

- There will be obvious blood loss from a wound or the victim will appear severely dehydrated from vomiting, diarrhea or sweating.
- The skin may be pale, cool, or clammy.
- The pulse is weak and rapid (greater than 100 beats per minute), or even undetectable.
- Breathing may be shallow and rapid, or irregular.
- Mental status may be altered (the victim may be confused, restless, or combative).

TREATMENT

1. Stop any bleeding by applying direct pressure to the bleeding site (see p. 24).
2. Keep the victim lying down, covered, and warm. Remember to insulate him from the ground.
3. Splint all broken bones (see p. 77). If the femur (thigh bone) is broken, apply and maintain constant traction.
4. After the bleeding has been stopped, elevate the victim's legs so that gravity can help improve the blood supply to the heart and brain. You can do this simply by having the victim recline on a slope with his feet uphill or elevate his legs on a pile of packs.

5. If the victim is alert, oriented, and not vomiting, give him small sips of cool fluid to drink.

6. Evacuate the victim as soon as possible to a medical facility.

💣 Internal Hypovolemic Shock

SIGNS AND SYMPTOMS

- Same as above except there is no external sign of blood loss. The victim may have a painful and tender belly from internal bleeding, or signs and symptoms of a broken pelvis or femur (thigh bone) (see p. 83).

TREATMENT

1. Keep the victim lying flat, covered, and warm. Remember to insulate him from the ground. Avoid unnecessary movement.

2. Do **not** elevate the victim's legs.

3. Splint all broken bones (see p. 77). If the femur (thigh bone) is broken, apply and maintain constant traction.

4. Do not give the victim anything to eat or drink.

5. Evacuate the victim as soon as possible to a medical facility.

💣 Cardiogenic Shock

SIGNS AND SYMPTOMS

- The victim may have chest pain and be short of breath.
- The victim will usually be uncomfortable lying flat because it can increase his shortness of breath.
- The skin may be pale, cool, or clammy.
- The pulse is weak and rapid (greater than 100 beats per minute) or even undetectable.
- Breathing is usually rapid and labored.
- Mental status may be altered (the victim may be confused, restless, or combative).
- The victim may have engorged or distended neck veins, or swollen ankles.

TREATMENT

1. Allow the victim to rest in his most comfortable position. He may be most comfortable with his head and shoulders raised slightly.

2. Do **not** elevate the victim's legs.

3. Do not give the victim anything to eat or drink.

4. Evacuate the victim as soon as possible to a medical facility.

💣 Spinal Shock

SIGNS AND SYMPTOMS

- The victim is paralyzed and can not move either his legs or both his arms and legs.

- The skin may be warm and flushed instead of pale and cool.
- The pulse rate is normal or even slow (50 to 70 beats per minute), but may feel weak or faint.
- Breathing may be shallow, rapid, or irregular.
- Mental status may be altered (the victim may be confused, restless, or combative).
- A male victim with spinal shock may have priapism (sustained penile erection).

TREATMENT

1. Do not move the victim unless it is necessary to do so for his safety. Keep him lying flat, and immobilize the head, neck, and body using spine precautions (see p. 29).
2. Keep the victim covered, and warm. Logroll the victim (see fig. 1) and place insulation between his back and the ground.
3. If the victim is alert, oriented, and not vomiting, give him small sips of cool fluid to drink.
4. Evacuate the victim as soon as possible to a medical facility. Professional evacuation is recommended to prevent any movement of the spine.

☀ Anaphylactic Shock

SIGNS AND SYMPTOMS

- The victim may develop hives (red, raised welts) on the skin, or the skin may just look red and be warm to the touch.
- The victim may have wheezing, chest tightness, and shortness of breath.
- The soft tissues of the throat, larynx, or windpipe may swell, making it difficult or impossible for the person to swallow or breathe.
- The pulse is weak and rapid (greater than 100 beats per minute), or even undetectable.
- Breathing may be shallow and rapid, or irregular.
- Mental status may be altered (the victim may be confused, restless, or combative).

TREATMENT

For treatment of anaphylactic shock, see Chapter 30.

Psychogenic Shock

SIGNS AND SYMPTOMS

- The victim has a fainting spell and may be temporarily unconscious.
- The pulse rate is normal or even slow (50 to 70 beats per minute), but may feel weak or be difficult to find.
- Breathing may be shallow, rapid, or irregular.

TREATMENT

1. Keep the victim lying flat, covered, and warm. Remember to insulate him from the ground.
2. Elevate the victim's legs so that gravity can help improve the blood supply to the heart and brain. You can do this simply by having the victim recline on a slope with his feet uphill or by placing a pile of packs under his legs.
3. If the victim is alert, oriented, and not vomiting, give him small sips of cool fluid to drink.

☀ Septic Shock

SIGNS AND SYMPTOMS

- The victim is suffering from a severe infection and will likely have a fever.
- The skin may be warm and flushed.
- The pulse is weak and rapid (greater than 100 beats per minute), or even undetectable.
- Breathing may be shallow, rapid, or irregular.
- Mental status may be altered (the victim may be confused, restless, or combative).

TREATMENT

1. Keep the victim lying down, covered, and warm. Remember to insulate him from the ground.
2. Elevate the victim's legs so that gravity can help improve the blood supply to the heart and brain. You can do this simply by having the victim recline on a slope with his feet uphill or by placing a pile of packs under his legs.
3. If the victim is alert, oriented, and not vomiting, give him small sips of cool fluid to drink.
4. Administer antibiotics if available (see Appendix B).
5. Evacuate the victim as soon as possible to a medical facility.

CHAPTER 3

Head Injuries

YOU CAN SUSTAIN A HEAD INJURY either during a fall or when something falls onto your head. The trauma sustained during a fall increases in direct proportion to the distance you fall. Falling 12 feet onto rock, for example, will produce a maximum velocity of 28 feet per second and an impact force of about 48 g's (that's 48 times the force of gravity; 1 g is what we normally feel while standing on the earth's surface). Falling from 24 feet will allow you to reach a velocity of 39 feet per second and experience an impact force of 95 g's. Most trauma centers classify a fall of 15 feet or greater as a major trauma. Falls from greater than 72 feet are usually fatal.

Each year in the United States, approximately 2 million people suffer head injuries. Of these, approximately 100,000 die and 90,000 become permanently disabled. In the backcountry, a head injury can be compounded by environmental factors, such as hypothermia (see p. 164), and the length of time it takes to get help.

PREVENTION

The most important factor in preventing a head injury is wearing a helmet. Helmets protect the head and brain by absorbing and dispersing the traumatic forces at the site of impact. To be effective, helmets must be properly fitted and tightly secured in place.

☀WHEN TO WORRY
Head Injuries

If any *one* **of the following signs or symptoms occur after a blow to the head, evacuate the victim as soon as possible** (see Appendix C).
- Headache that progressively worsens.
- The victim's level of consciousness gradually deteriorates from alertness to

apathy, drowsiness, or unconsciousness. The victim may also exhibit bizarre or unusual behavior.

- Repetitive or projectile vomiting (vomiting that shoots out under pressure).
- One pupil becomes significantly larger than the other.
- Bleeding from the nose or an ear without direct injury to those areas, or a clear watery fluid draining from the ear or nose.
- Bruising behind the ears or around **both** eyes, when there is no direct injury to those areas.
- Seizures (convulsions).

   Note: The most important single sign to look for in the evaluation of a head-injured victim is a changing state of consciousness or alertness.

ASSESSMENT OF THE HEAD-INJURED VICTIM

1. Perform a "primary survey" in which you look for life-threatening conditions, such as a blocked airway (see p. 16) or severe bleeding (see p. 24) and attempt to correct the problem. Speak loudly to the victim. A response indicates that he is breathing and has a pulse.
2. If the victim is unconscious, begin with the ABC's of resuscitation (see p. 22).
3. In an unconscious victim, the airway can become obstructed when the muscles of the tongue and throat go limp, which allows the tongue to fall back and obstruct the airway. Open the airway, using the jaw-thrust maneuver (see fig. 4) to prevent unnecessary movement of the neck. Keep in mind that if the forces that produced the head injury were powerful enough to cause loss of consciousness, they were also strong enough to potentially damage the cervical spine and the spinal cord within it.
4. In the head-injured victim, the airway may also be obstructed by vomitus or broken teeth. Make a quick inspection of the victim's mouth. If necessary, logroll the victim (see fig. 1) to clear the mouth without twisting the spine.

CLASSIFICATION OF HEAD INJURIES

For purposes of backcountry diagnosis and treatment, head injuries can be subdivided into three groups:

1. Prolonged unconsciousness (more than 5 to 10 minutes)
2. Brief loss of consciousness (1 to 2 minutes)
3. No loss of consciousness

💣☀ Prolonged Unconsciousness

Prolonged unconsciousness is a sign of significant brain injury. A blow to the head sends shock waves that temporarily disrupt brain function. The longer the victim remains unconscious, the worse the brain injury is likely to be. The force of the blow can fracture the skull, bruise the brain, or cause severe bleeding inside the brain from torn blood vessels. The brain responds much like any other bruised or bleeding body part—it swells. The problem with swelling in the head, however, is that the brain sits inside a cramped container. There is no room for the brain to expand, and intracranial pressure rapidly increases.

Increased intracranial pressure is bad for the brain for several reasons. The increased pressure makes it difficult for the heart to pump enough blood to the brain. This is a major catastrophe for the brain which depends on a constant supply of blood to bring it oxygen and other nutrients. Another damaging effect of increased intracranial pressure is a condition known as herniation. If the pressure within the skull rises high enough, it can force parts of the brain downward, through the base of the skull, causing severe damage to the brain structures and ultimately death.

SIGNS AND SYMPTOMS

- Loss of consciousness for more than 5 to 10 minutes.
- One or more of the signs or symptoms in the "When to Worry" box for head injuries may be present (see above).

TREATMENT

1. Immediately evacuate the victim to a medical facility (see Appendix C). During transportation, be extremely careful to keep the victim's neck immobilized (see p. 68) and to keep his head pointed uphill on sloping terrain. Be prepared to logroll the victim onto his side (see fig. 1) if he vomits.
2. Continually monitor the victim's airway for signs of obstruction (listen for noisy or labored breathing) and a decreasing respiratory rate.

Brief Loss of Consciousness

Brief loss of consciousness does not usually produce any permanent brain damage (this type of injury is typically referred to as a concussion).

SIGNS AND SYMPTOMS

- The victim wakes after 1 or 2 minutes and gradually regains normal mental status and physical abilities, except that he generally cannot recall what happened to him and asks the same questions repeatedly.

TREATMENT

1. Observe the victim closely for any of the signs and symptoms on the "When to Worry" list for head injuries (see above).
2. If such symptoms appear, evacuate the victim to a medical facility for evaluation (see Appendix C).

No Loss of Consciousness

If an individual hits his head but never loses consciousness, the consequences are rarely serious.

SIGNS AND SYMPTOMS

- Mild headache.
- Bleeding from a scalp wound.
- Large bump on the head.

TREATMENT

1. Evacuation is not necessary unless the victim develops a sign or symptom on the "When to Worry" list for head injuries (see above).
2. Treat a bump on the head, which is a localized swelling from a bruise to the scalp, by applying ice or cold packs.
3. Administer acetaminophen (Tylenol®) 500-1,000 mg for pain.
4. See below for treatment of scalp lacerations.

●᙮WHEN TO WORRY
Skull Fractures

Skull fractures are commonly open, or compound, fractures—that is, the overlying skin at the fracture site has been punctured or cut, thus exposing the brain to infection.

All skull fractures are potentially serious and the victim should be evacuated to a medical facility as soon as possible (see Appendix C).

SIGNS AND SYMPTOMS

- The skull feels uneven when scalp is touched.
- Blood or clear fluid drains from the ears or nose without direct trauma to those areas.
- Black-and-blue discoloration around both eyes ("raccoon eyes") or behind an ear.

TREATMENT

1. Allow the victim to walk if he can do so without difficulty, but keep a close eye and hand on him in the event that he begins to lose his balance or coordination. If the victim is dizzy, lightheaded, confused, uncoordinated, or not acting normally, he should be carried from the wilderness or evacuated by professional rescuers, after immobilizing the spine.
2. If blood is draining from the ears, place a piece of gauze or cotton in the ear canal.
3. Control any bleeding from the scalp with direct pressure.

Scalp Lacerations (Cuts)

Scalp lacerations are common with head injuries and tend to bleed profusely because of the scalp's rich blood supply. Fortunately, bleeding can usually be stopped by applying direct pressure to the bleeding site.

SIGNS AND SYMPTOMS
* Profuse bleeding from the scalp.

TREATMENT
Using protective gloves to protect yourself from possible blood-borne infections, stop the bleeding by applying direct pressure to the wound (see p. 24). Use whatever clean material is available, and then, as time allows, replace it with 4 by 4 inch sterile gauze pads to hold the pressure. The idea is not to soak up blood with a big wad of bandage material, but to apply focused and firm pressure directly on the bleeding site. It may be necessary to hold the pressure for up to 30 minutes before the bleeding stops entirely.

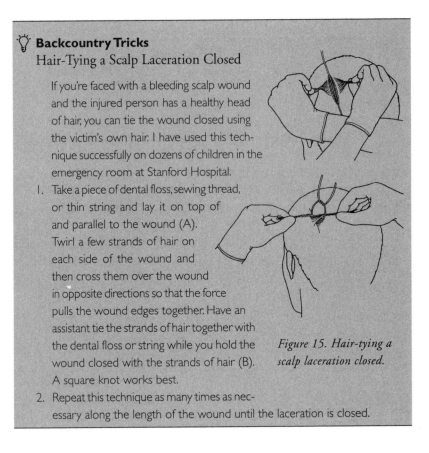

☿ Backcountry Tricks
Hair-Tying a Scalp Laceration Closed

If you're faced with a bleeding scalp wound and the injured person has a healthy head of hair, you can tie the wound closed using the victim's own hair. I have used this technique successfully on dozens of children in the emergency room at Stanford Hospital.

1. Take a piece of dental floss, sewing thread, or thin string and lay it on top of and parallel to the wound (A). Twirl a few strands of hair on each side of the wound and then cross them over the wound in opposite directions so that the force pulls the wound edges together. Have an assistant tie the strands of hair together with the dental floss or string while you hold the wound closed with the strands of hair (B). A square knot works best.

Figure 15. Hair-tying a scalp laceration closed.

2. Repeat this technique as many times as necessary along the length of the wound until the laceration is closed.

CHAPTER 4

Headache

AT LEAST 60 PERCENT OF THE population will have a significant headache at some time in their lives, and it is one of the most common reasons for visiting a physician. Headaches can stem from innumerable causes, including tension and stress, migraine, dehydration, altitude illness (see p. 158), alcohol hangover, carbon monoxide poisoning, brain tumors, strokes (see p. 203), aneurysms, intracranial bleeds, fever, flu, meningitis and other infectious diseases, high blood pressure, sinus infections (see p. 207), and dental problems (see p. 55). Suddenly going "cold turkey" on caffeine during a backpacking trip, especially if you regularly drink more than three cups of coffee a day, can also precipitate a headache.

PREVENTION
Dehydration is a common cause of headaches in the wilderness. You need to drink at least 4 quarts of fluid a day when backpacking. A good barometer of your hydration status is the color of your urine. If it is not clear like gin, then you are not drinking enough.

☀WHEN TO WORRY
Headaches

Some headaches may signal a life-threatening illness. If you experience *any* **of the following signs or symptoms, get to a medical facility as soon as possible:**

- The headache is the worst of your life and came on very suddenly and severely (possible aneurysm or intracranial bleeding).
- Your arms and legs on one side are weak, numb, or paralyzed, or one side of your face appears droopy (possible stroke—see p. 203).
- You are unable to talk or express yourself clearly (possible stroke).

- You have a fever, stiff neck, or any rash (possible meningitis).
- Your headache grows steadily worse over time (possible brain tumor).
- You have repetitive vomiting (increased intracranial pressure).
- Seizures or convulsions develop (severe brain dysfunction).
- The pain does not go away within 24 hours.

Tension Headache
(Stress or Muscle Contraction Headache)

This is the most common type of headache and affects people of all ages. The pain is related to continuous contractions of the muscles of the head and neck.

SIGNS AND SYMPTOMS

- Pain can last from 30 minutes to 7 days.
- The headache is often described as tight or viselike, and felt on both sides, especially in the back of the head and neck.
- The pain is *not* usually made worse by walking, climbing, or performing physical activity.
- Sensitivity to light may occur, but nausea and vomiting are not usually present.

TREATMENT

1. Loosen any tight-fitting pack straps or hat, and adjust your pack so that it rides comfortably.
2. Ibuprofen (Motrin®) 600 mg every 8 hours with food or acetaminophen (Tylenol®) 1,000 mg every 4 to 6 hours may help relieve the discomfort.

 Backcountry Tricks
Relieving Tension Headaches

Spasm or soreness of the sternocleidomastoid and trapezius muscles, which run down the neck and shoulders from the head, is often the source of tension headaches. Placing a rolled-up towel or pillow directly under the back of the neck while sleeping on your back may help to relieve spasm in these muscles. Acupressure, massage, and stretching of these muscles can also help relieve a tension headache. Muscle relaxers such as diazepam (Valium®) 5mg every 6 hours may provide short-term relief.

Migraine Headache

The term *migraine* is often used as a catch-all phrase but should be reserved for those headaches that show specific patterns.

SIGNS AND SYMPTOMS
- These are recurrent headaches that involve usually (but not always) one side of the head and are associated with nausea, vomiting, and sensitivity to light.
- Walking or physical exertion makes the pain worse.
- About 15 percent of people with migraine headaches will experience an aura (flashing lights, distorted shapes and colors, blurred vision, or other visual apparitions) prior to the onset of the headache.

TREATMENT
1. Ibuprofen (Motrin®) 600 mg every 8 hours with food and caffeine-containing beverages like coffee may help relieve symptoms, especially if taken early.
2. Stronger prescription medications like acetaminophen (Tylenol®) with codeine (one to two pills every 4 to 6 hours) and sumitriptan (Imitrex®) 6 mg may be needed.
3. Lying down in the shade with a cool compress on the forehead may be helpful.

Dehydration Headache

Headache can be an early sign of dehydration (see p. 174).
SIGNS AND SYMPTOMS
- The pain is felt on both sides of the head.
- The pain is usually made worse when the victim stands from a lying position.

TREATMENT
1. Resting and drinking at least 1 to 2 quarts of water should relieve the pain.
2. Ibuprofen (Motrin®) 600 mg every 8 hours with food or acetaminophen (Tylenol®) 1,000 mg every 4 to 6 hours may also be helpful.

CHAPTER 5

Eye Problems

APPROXIMATELY 1.5 MILLION EYE injuries occur in the United States each year; about 50,000 result in some degree of visual loss. Since trauma to the eye is so common, and since the potential consequences are so serious, it is important to know how to diagnose and treat eye injuries in the wilderness.

The eyeball sits within a bony cavity of the skull called the eye socket or orbit. The parts of the eyeball most likely to be injured or subject to illness in the backcountry are:

- The **cornea:** a clear, transparent, thin window-like covering over the front of the eye.
- The **conjunctiva:** a delicate mucous membrane that covers the white part of the eyeball and lines the undersurface of the eyelids.
- The **lens:** a lenticular structure which sits behind the cornea and focuses light onto the retina.
- The **retina:** a thin movie-screen-like structure that makes up the back wall of the eye.

PREVENTION

The cornea, retina, and lens of the eye are all vulnerable to damage from sunlight, both in the short term and from repeated exposure. For example, short-term exposure to ultraviolet light can produce a sunburn-like effect to the cornea leading to a severe form of corneal abrasion. Chronic or long-term exposure of the cornea to ultraviolet light produces cataracts.

Always wear sunglasses in the backcountry to prevent sun damage to the cornea, retina, and lens. Sunglasses should protect against no less than 99 percent of the sun's ultraviolet radiation. When traveling in the snow, especially at altitudes above 5,000 feet, use side shields on your sunglasses to block out reflected light from the snow. If you forget or lose your sunglasses, you can always improvise.

Backcountry Tricks
Improvising Sunglasses

You can improvise a pair of "sunglasses" that will help protect your
eyes from ultraviolet light by cutting
small slits in a piece of cardboard (you
can use one side of a cracker or ce-
real box) or in a piece of duct tape folded
back over onto itself (fig. 16). The slits should
*Figure 16. Improvised
sunglasses.*

be just wide enough to see through, and no larger than the diameter of
your eye. Tape or tie these "sunglasses" around your head to minimize the
amount of ultraviolet light hitting your eyes.

 WHEN TO WORRY
Eye Trauma

**Seek medical care immediately if the victim has an eye injury
and any of the following signs or symptoms:**
• The injury does not heal spontaneously in 2 days.
• There is increasing redness, pain, or swelling.
• Greenish fluid begins to drain from the eye.
• The victim's vision worsens.

Ruptured Eyeball

A blow to the face can rupture the eyeball and fracture one or more of the skull
bones that form the orbit. The eyeball can also be ruptured by an object that is
stuck or driven into the eye. A ruptured eyeball is a medical emergency that requires immediate evacuation for surgery on the eye (see Appendix C).

SIGNS AND SYMPTOMS
• Vision loss, ranging from blurred sight to total blindness.
• Pain.
• Dilated pupil that does not react to changes in light.
• Blood in the eye.
• The fluid in the eye may have leaked out, giving it a collapsed or flattened
  appearance.

- With an orbital bone fracture, the victim may have double vision and feel numb above the eyebrow or over the cheek.

TREATMENT

1. **Do not remove** a foreign object that penetrates the eye, as this may cause further injury. Stabilize the object in place by securing rolled-up dressings on either side of the object and taping them together. Another technique is to take several layers of 4 by 4 inch gauze pads and cut a hole in the center large enough to pass over the foreign object without putting pressure on it. Then cover the eye with a paper cone, cup, or other protective object and secure this in place with a bandage (fig. 17). Be careful not to put pressure on the eye.
2. If the eyeball is ruptured, but there is no penetrating object, cover the eye with a paper cup or cone and secure this in place with a bandage. Remember not to put any pressure on the eye.
3. Patch the other eye to reduce eye movements (when one eye moves, the other moves with it), unless the victim has to walk out under his own power.
4. Administer oral antibiotics if you have them available (see Appendix B). Do not place any drops, medicine or fluid directly into the eye.
5. Evacuate the victim to a medical facility as soon as possible.

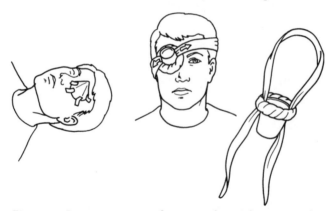

Figure 17. Protective covering for ruptured eye. This protects the eye without putting any pressure on the eyeball.

☀ Hyphema (Blood Behind the Cornea)

A blow to the eye can produce bleeding behind the cornea without rupturing the eyeball. If the bleeding is severe, the victim can eventually become blind.

SIGNS AND SYMPTOMS

- A visible layer of blood will settle behind the cornea and be noticeable 6 to 8 hours after injury.

TREATMENT

1. The eye should be patched closed with a 4 by 4 inch sterile gauze pad and tape.
2. Evacuate the victim immediately to medical care (see Appendix C), keeping the head elevated and in an upright position.

💣 Retinal Detachment

Trauma to the eye can also cause the retina to become detached from the back of the eye.

SIGNS AND SYMPTOMS

- Sudden, painless loss of vision in one eye.
- Light flashes or floating spots may appear in the victim's field of vision or the victim may describe the sensation that a dark curtain is obstructing part of his field of view.

TREATMENT

A detached retina requires surgical repair. Seek immediate medical care.

Scratched Eye (Corneal Abrasion)

The clear covering over the front of the eye is called the cornea. It is easily scratched or abraded.

SIGNS AND SYMPTOMS

- The victim feels as if he has sand in his eye.
- The eye will usually appear bloodshot.
- The eye waters.
- Slight blurring of vision.
- Intense pain, made worse by blinking the eyes.
- Sensitivity to light.
- Close inspection of the cornea may show a slight irregularity on its surface.

TREATMENT

1. Check the eyes carefully for foreign material, making sure to examine under the upper lid. To examine under the upper lid, have the victim look downward as you grasp the eyelashes with your thumb and finger. Using a cotton-tipped applicator, place the end of the applicator in the middle of the upper lid. Using the applicator as a fulcrum, pull the lid forward and upward, causing it to fold back over the applicator (inside out) exposing the undersurface of the lid (fig. 18). (See treatment for superficial foreign bodies below.)
2. Cool compresses may help relieve some of the irritation.
3. If available, apply antibiotic eyedrops such as tobramycin (Tobrex®) 2 to 3 drops every 2 to 3 hours while awake, for 2 to 3 days.
4. Administer pain medication such as hydrocodone and acetaminophen

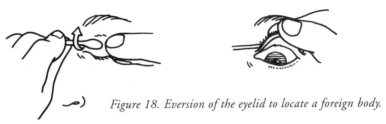

Figure 18. Eversion of the eyelid to locate a foreign body.

(Vicodin®, see Appendix B) and have the victim rest his eyes as much as possible. Most of the time, the injury heals itself in 1 to 2 days.

5. Patching the eye with an eye patch or a bandage for 24 hours may help to reduce pain. If an eye patch or other bandage is not available, the eye can be taped closed or the victim can wear sunglasses (for improvised sunglasses, see fig. 16). An eye should not be patched closed if there is any sign of infection (yellow or green discharge from the eye, swelling, fever).

💡 **Backcountry Tricks**
Using a Tea Bag to Relieve Eye Pain

Drops of tea squeezed from a cool, nonherbal tea bag may help to soothe the eye and relieve pain.

Snow Blindness

Snow blindness is a sunburn of the eye from intense ultraviolet radiation at high altitude or while traveling in the snow. The sunburn results in corneal abrasion. Unfortunately one is unaware that the injury is occurring until it is too late, because the signs and symptoms of snow blindness are delayed by about 6 hours from the time of exposure to the light.

SIGNS AND SYMPTOMS
See Scratched Eye (above).

TREATMENT
See Scratched Eye (above).

Subconjunctival Hemorrhage

Subconjunctival hemorrhage sometimes occurs after physical exertion, coughing, or strangulation but is not a serious condition.

SIGNS AND SYMPTOMS
• Blood clots (or what looks like a red film) on the white part of the eye.

TREATMENT

No treatment is necessary, as the hemorrhage will resorb by itself over a few weeks' time.

Superficial Foreign Bodies

Most foreign bodies in the eye are tiny particles which can easily be removed. If the foreign body is imbedded in the eye and can not be removed by irrigation or with the corner of a moistened cloth or cotton swab, leave it in place and seek medical attention as soon as possible. Do not attempt to remove a foreign body with any sharp or stiff object, as this can produce more damage.

SIGNS AND SYMPTOMS

- The victim may notice a "spot" in his vision and feel as if he has a piece of sand in his eye.
- The foreign body should be visible when you look into the eye with a bright light.

TREATMENT

1. If a foreign body enters the eye, but is not imbedded in the eyeball, attempt to remove it by irrigating the eye with a stream of disinfected water.
2. If irrigation does not remove the foreign body, carefully attempt to lift the material out gently with a moistened cotton swab or cloth.
3. Sometimes the foreign body will lodge underneath the upper eyelid. Examine under the eyelid by everting it (see fig. 18).
4. After objects are removed from the eye, victims often report feeling as if something is still in their eye. This is usually caused by small scratches on the surface of the cornea. Treat the same as for a scratched eye (see above).

 Backcountry Tricks
Irrigating the Eyes

Pour disinfected water into a clean sandwich or garbage bag and puncture the bottom of the bag with a safety pin. Squeeze the top of the bag firmly to create an irrigation stream, which can then be directed into the eye.

Conjunctivitis (Pink Eye)

Conjunctivitis is an infection or inflammation of the conjunctiva, a mucous membrane that covers the white part of the eyeball and lines the undersurface of the eyelids. It can be caused by a virus or bacteria, or by allergic or toxic agents. The most common cause is viral infection, and the condition is often associated with other cold symptoms.

SIGNS AND SYMPTOMS
- Red, itchy eye(s).
- Yellow or green discharge from the eyes.
- Crusted eyelashes.
- Swollen eyelids.

TREATMENT
1. Irrigate the eye with disinfected water.
2. Apply antibiotic eyedrops, such as tobramycin (Tobrex®), 2 to 3 drops every 2 to 3 hours while awake (see Appendix B).

Styes or Abscesses

A sty is an infection or abscess of the sebaceous gland of an eyelash or eyelash follicle. It usually begins as a red nodule that progresses into a painful pustule within a few days.

SIGNS AND SYMPTOMS
- Swollen, red, painful eyelid.
- Eventually a pustle forms on the edge of the eyelid.

TREATMENT
1. When a sty begins to develop, apply warm, moist compresses to the eyelid for 30 minutes four times a day until the sty either disappears or enlarges and comes to a head. If it comes to a head, but does not drain spontaneously, seek medical attention.
2. If the victim is more than 48 hours from medical care and the infection is progressing to include the cheek or forehead, lance the sty carefully with a scalpel or pin. (Make sure you sterilize the pin by either boiling it in water for 5 minutes, heating it over a flame, or putting it in Betadine®.) Start antibiotic therapy with erythromycin, or cephalexin (Keflex®) (see Appendix B).

CHAPTER 6

Nosebleeds

BLEEDING FROM THE NOSE CAN occur for many reasons, including colds and sinus infections (see p. 207), dry air such as is found on airplanes, trauma, allergies, high blood pressure, liver disease, leukemia, and hemophilia. The source of bleeding can either be from blood vessels in the front or the back of the nose. Bleeding from the front of the nose is usually easy to stop, while bleeding from the back of the nose can be difficult to control and can even be life threatening.

☀WHEN TO WORRY
Bleeding from the Back of the Nose

Bleeding from the back of the nose is a serious problem, as the victim can lose a significant amount of blood, and it may be difficult or impossible to stop the bleeding in the backcountry.

SIGNS AND SYMPTOMS
- Blood often drains from both nostrils and down the back of the throat.
- Pinching the nostrils tightly together does not stop the bleeding, and the victim continues to feel blood drain down the back of the throat.

TREATMENT

Evacuate the victim to a medical facility as soon as possible (see Appendix C).

Bleeding from the Front of the Nose

Ninety percent of all nosebleeds originate from the front of the nose.

SIGNS AND SYMPTOMS
- Blood usually drains from one nostril, and can be controlled by pinching the nostrils between the fingers.
- If blood continues to drain down the back of the throat while the nostrils are pinched tightly, then the bleeding is from the back of the nose.

TREATMENT
1. Pinch the soft part of the nostrils together between your fingers and hold it firmly for at least 15 to 20 minutes.
2. If the bleeding stops when you pinch the nostrils but resumes when you let go after 20 minutes of firm pressure, you may need to pack the front of the nose (see below).

💡 **Backcountry Tricks**

Packing the Front of the Nose

1. If available, first insert a piece of cotton or gauze soaked with a blood-vessel constrictor (such as Afrin® or NeoSynephrine® nasal spray or even tea from a herbal tea bag) into the nose. Leave it in place for 5 minutes and then remove it.

2. Cut a large gauze pad or soft cotton cloth into a thin continuous strip (to completely pack the nasal cavity of an adult, you will need about 3 feet of packing).

3. Coat the strip with petroleum jelly (Vaseline®) or antibiotic ointment.

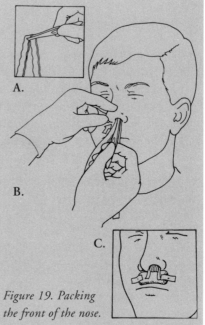

Figure 19. Packing the front of the nose.

4. Beginning with the middle of the strip (A), gently pack it into the nostril, using tweezers or a thin twig so that both ends of the packing material remain outside of the nasal cavity (B). This will keep the ends of the packing from going down the back of the throat. Tape a piece of rolled-up gauze under the nose to secure the packing in place (C). Leave the pack in for 24 to 48 hours, then gently remove it (fig. 19).

5. If bleeding starts again, repack the nostril.

6. Packing the nose will block sinus drainage and predispose the victim to a sinus infection (see p. 207). Administer oral antibiotics, such as trimethoprim/sulfamethoxazole (Septra®, Bactrim®), amoxicillin clavulanate (Augmentin®), cephalexin (Keflex®), or amoxicillin (Amoxil®) until the packing is removed.

CHAPTER 7

Dental Emergencies

DENTAL PROBLEMS ARE QUITE COMMON in the backcountry. I know several mountaineers who either broke a tooth or dislodged a filling after biting into a hard or frozen energy bar. As you ascend in altitude, any unfilled cavity lurking in a tooth (and which produces no discomfort at sea level) may suddenly be unmasked by the expansion of air in the cavity at higher elevations and produce excruciating pain.

Always use protective gloves when working in the mouth to prevent the spread of infectious diseases.

PREVENTION

A visit to your dentist before any extended trip may save a lot of aggravation and pain from a festering tooth that decides to act up in the middle of your outing. Teeth should be brushed and flossed after every meal, even when camping. Game meat, such as moose or rabbit, can often be stringy and stick between the teeth. Any residue should be removed by flossing as it can irritate the gums and lead to infection. Carrying a few dental items in your first-aid kit, such as Cavit® temporary filling and dental wax, and knowing how to use them can prevent a lot of suffering.

 Backcountry Tricks
Improvising a Toothbrush

If a toothbrush is forgotten or lost, take the end of a thin green twig and chew it until it is soft and fibery. Use the fibrous end of the twig as a toothbrush to clean the gums and between the teeth.

Dental Infections and Abscesses

When a tooth decays or is chipped, infection may occur at the gum line or at the base of the root. An abscess (pus pocket) may form at the base of the tooth and create pressure, swelling, and severe pain. Dental infections occasionally spread beyond the tooth to the floor of the mouth, the face, and the neck producing severe illness.

SIGNS AND SYMPTOMS

- Severe, usually throbbing dental pain associated with swelling in the gum line at the base of the tooth.
- Tapping the offending tooth causes pain, but the tooth is not usually sensitive to hot or cold.
- Fever may be present.
- If the infection spreads beyond the tooth, the cheek and face on the affected side will appear swollen. If the infection spreads to the floor of the mouth, the victim may have difficulty opening his mouth, swallowing, or even breathing.

TREATMENT

1. Administer oral antibiotics such as penicillin 500 mg every 6 hours (see Appendix B).
2. Rinse the mouth with warm salt water every 4 hours.
3. Administer pain medication such as ibuprofen (Motrin® 800 mg every 8 hours with food) or hydrocodone and acetaminophen (two Vicodin® tablets every 4 to 6 hours) as needed.
4. Make every effort to locate a dentist as soon as possible since dental infections can spread and cause serious illness. Extraction of the offending tooth, or root canal therapy is usually required to completely treat the infection.

Knocked-out (Avulsed) Tooth

If a tooth is completely knocked out, it may be salvageable if replaced into the socket within 30 to 60 minutes.

SIGNS AND SYMPTOMS

- The tooth has been totally avulsed from its socket and can often be found in the victim's mouth or on the ground.
- The tooth itself should be in one piece and not broken.
- There may be bleeding from the socket and around the gum.

TREATMENT

1. Clean the debris off the tooth by rinsing gently (do not scrub!) with either sterile saline solution (see p. 116), milk, or disinfected water and gently replace the tooth into the socket. *Note: Handle the tooth only by the crown, not by the root. The root is very fragile and if it dies the tooth will not reimplant.*

2. If you cannot replace the tooth immediately, store it in a container containing a sterile saline solution, milk, or saliva, in that order of preference.

3. Bleeding can be controlled with direct pressure and by the use of a tea bag.

 Backcountry Tricks
Relieving Dental Pain and Bleeding with a Tea Bag

You can often relieve pain and bleeding from the mouth by placing a moistened nonherbal tea bag on the bleeding site or into the tooth socket that is bleeding. Leave it in place for 5 to 10 minutes.

Toothache

The common toothache is caused by inflammation of the dental pulp and is often associated with a cavity.

SIGNS AND SYMPTOMS

- Pain may be severe and intermittent and is made worse by hot or cold foods or liquids.

TREATMENT

1. If the offending cavity can be localized, apply a piece of cotton soaked with a topical anti-inflammatory agent such as eugenol (oil of cloves) over it.

2. Place a temporary filling material, such as Cavit®, zinc oxide and eugenol cement, or dental wax into the cavity or lost-filling site to protect the nerve and lessen its sensitivity to hot or cold liquids and food.

3. Administer pain medication such as ibuprofen (Motrin® 800 mg every 8 hours with food) or hydrocodone and acetaminophen (two Vicodin® tablets every 4 to 6 hours) as needed.

 Backcountry Tricks
Replacing a Lost Filling

Melt some candle wax and allow it to cool until it is just soft and pliable. Place the wax into the cavity or lost-filling site and smooth it out with your finger. Have the victim bite down to seat the wax in place, and remove any excess wax.

Loose Tooth

A tooth may be knocked loose and partially displaced within the socket. The tooth will usually survive, but may need to be splinted by a dentist.

SIGNS AND SYMPTOMS

- The tooth is in its normal position but rocks back and forth when touched.
- The tooth may be partially displaced from its normal position and sitting at an abnormal angle.

TREATMENT

1. Reposition the loose tooth with gentle, steady pressure.
2. Eat a soft diet to avoid any further trauma until the tooth heals.
3. See a dentist as soon as possible for definitive treatment.

CHAPTER 8

Chest Injuries

A BLOW TO THE CHEST USUALLY produces only mild pain from bruising of the muscles in the chest wall. A forceful blow to the chest may break one or more ribs, which can produce severe pain and sometimes injure the underlying lung. Occasionally a rib fracture or wound to the chest can lead to a life-threatening condition called a tension pneumothorax, in which the lung collapses and the victim is deprived of oxygen. **Anytime a victim experiences shortness of breath or difficulty breathing after a blow or wound to the chest, suspect an injury to the underlying lung and immediately evacuate the victim to a medical facility** (see Appendix C). 💣*

Broken Ribs

Generally speaking, a broken rib by itself is not a serious emergency. However, complications sometimes associated with a broken rib, such as a collapsed or bruised lung, can produce serious consequences. Broken ribs usually result from a direct blow to the chest, and are extremely painful.

SIGNS AND SYMPTOMS

- Pain in the chest that becomes worse when the victim takes a deep breath.
- A crackling or rattling sensation or sound can occasionally be detected when the broken rib is touched.
- Broken ribs usually occur along the side of the chest. Pushing on the sternum (breastbone), in front of the chest, while the victim lies on his back, will produce pain at the site where the rib is broken, instead of where you are pushing.

TREATMENT

It takes about 2 weeks for pain to subside and 4 to 6 weeks for the rib to heal.

1. Oral pain medication, such as ibuprofen (Motrin® 800 mg every 8 hours with food) or hydrocodone and acetaminophen (Vicodin® 1 to 2 tablets every 4 to 6 hours) will help reduce pain and make breathing easier.
2. Taping the chest over the broken rib may provide added relief from pain.

✸WHEN TO WORRY
Serious Complications That Can Occur with Broken Ribs

One end of a broken rib can sometimes be displaced inward and puncture the lung, producing a pneumothorax (see p. 60). A broken rib can also bruise the lung or predispose the victim to pneumonia (see p. 210). If a rib in the lower part of the chest is broken, it may injure the spleen or liver and cause severe internal bleeding.

If the victim develops any of the following signs or symptoms, or is suspected of having more than one broken rib, he should be immediately evacuated to a medical facility (see Appendix C).

- Shortness of breath.
- Difficulty breathing.
- Persistent cough.
- Fever.
- Abdominal pain.
- Dizziness or lightheadedness upon standing.

✸ Flail Chest

When three or more consecutive ribs on the same side of the chest are broken in two places, a free-floating segment called a "flail chest" can result. The flail segment will move in the opposite direction from the rest of the chest during breathing, thus making it hard for the victim to get enough air. In addition, the movement of broken ribs causes great pain, which further reduces the victim's abiltity to breathe. With a flail chest the underlying lung is usually bruised.

SIGNS AND SYMPTOMS

- The victim is usually in severe pain and experiences shortness of breath.
- The flail segment will move in the opposite direction from the rest of the chest during breathing. When the victim inhales, the section is sucked in. When he exhales, it is pushed out. (You can determine if this is happening by gently placing your hand on the victim's chest wall.)
- A cracking or rattling can be heard (or felt) when the area is touched.

TREATMENT

1. Immediately evacuate the victim to a medical facility (see Appendix C). A flail chest can be tolerated only for the first 24 to 48 hours, after which the victim will usually need to be put on a mechanical ventilator for a period of time to assist with breathing.

2. Place a bulky pad of dressings, rolled-up extra clothing, or a small pillow gently over the injured site, or have the victim splint his arm against the site to stabilize the flail segment and relieve some of the pain. Whatever object is used should be soft and lightweight. Use large strips of tape to hold the pad in place. Do not tape entirely around the chest as this will restrict breathing efforts. The main function of splinting an object against the injury is to make it less painful to breathe, not to stop movement of the chest or to restrict breathing.

3. If the victim is unable to walk, he should be transported lying on his back or on the injured side.

4. If the victim is severely short of breath and cannot get enough air, you may need to assist his breathing with mouth-to-mouth resuscitation (see p. 22). Time your breaths to the victim's breathing, and breathe gently to give him added air as he inhales.

Collapsed Lung (Pneumothorax)

A collapsed lung (pneumothorax) is a potentially life-threatening situation in which air enters the chest cavity surrounding the lung and compresses or "collapses" the lung. A pneumothorax can occur when a broken rib punctures the lung; when an outside object such as a knife penetrates the chest into the lung; or even spontaneously, when a weak point develops in the lung, permitting air to leak into the chest cavity. Depending on the severity of the pneumothorax, the situation can range from being so minor that it is not noticeable to becoming a threat to life.

SIGNS AND SYMPTOMS

- Sharp chest pain that may become worse with breathing.
- Shortness of breath or difficulty breathing.
- Reduced or absent breath sounds on the injured side.

TREATMENT

1. Evacuate the victim immediately to a medical facility and monitor closely for the development of a tension pneumothorax (see below).

2. If the victim is unable to walk, he should be transported lying on his back or on the injured side.

Tension Pneumothorax

A pneumothorax can progress to a tension pneumothorax if air continues to leak into the chest cavity and cannot escape. Pressure soon builds up, compressing the lungs and heart, which can rapidly lead to death.

SIGNS AND SYMPTOMS

- Labored breathing.
- Cyanosis (bluish skin discoloration).

- Signs of shock (weak, rapid pulse, rapid breathing, fear, pale and moist skin, confusion) (see p. 33).
- Distended jugular (neck) veins.
- Diminished or absent breath sounds on the injured side (place your ear on the chest wall of the victim).
- Tapping on the injured side may produce a drumlike sound.
- Bubbles of air may be felt or heard (crackling or "Rice Krispies" sounds) on touching the chest wall or neck.

TREATMENT
1. Evacuate the victim immediately to a medical facility (see Appendix C).

💣 Open ("Sucking") Chest Wound

If an object such as a bullet or knife enters the chest, a wound that extends into the lung can occur. As the victim breathes, a sucking sound can often be heard as air passes in and out through the hole. The lung will usually partially collapse, producing a pneumothorax (see above). The wound can also allow bacteria to get into the lung and produce a severe infection. **A penetrating chest wound below the nipple line may also have produced an injury to an abdominal organ, such as the spleen or liver** (see Chapter 9).

SIGNS AND SYMPTOMS
- Painful and difficult breathing.
- A sucking sound may be heard each time the victim inhales.
- Bubbles may be seen at the wound site when the victim exhales.
- Bubbles of air may be felt or heard (crackling sounds) on touching the chest wall near the injury.
- The victim may develop signs of a tension pneumothorax (see above).

TREATMENT
1. Seal the opening immediately with any airtight substance (see below), such as plastic food wrap, a plastic sandwich baggy, or garbage bag (anything plastic will do) and cover the dressing with a 4 by 4 inch sterile gauze pad. Tape this combination down on three sides to make a flutter valve. When the victim inhales, the free edge will seal against the skin. As he exhales, the free edge will break loose from the skin and allow any build-up of air in the chest cavity to escape (fig. 20).
2. If an object is stuck in the chest, do not remove it. Place airtight material next to the skin around it, and stabilize it with bulky dressings or pads. Several layers of dressings, clothing, or handkerchiefs placed on the sides of the object will help stabilize it.
3. Immediately evacuate the victim to a medical facility (see Appendix C).

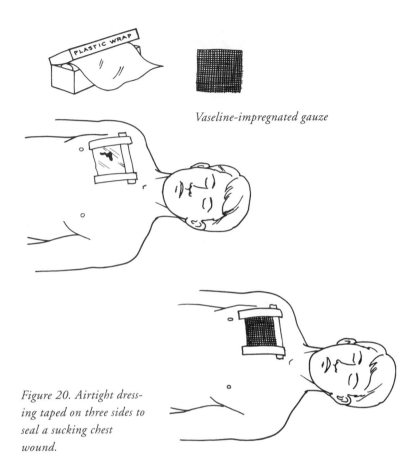

Vaseline-impregnated gauze

Figure 20. Airtight dressing taped on three sides to seal a sucking chest wound.

♀ Backcountry Tricks
Improvising an Airtight Dressing

You can improvise an airtight dressing from a sterile 4 by 4 inch gauze pad impregnated with petroleum jelly (Vaseline®), honey, or antibiotic ointment. Clean plastic food wrap will also work. Tape the dressing in place on three sides only.

CHAPTER 9

Abdominal Injuries

ABDOMINAL ORGANS ARE EITHER solid or hollow. When solid abdominal organs, such as the spleen or liver are injured, they bleed internally. Internal blood loss can cause the victim to go into shock (see p. 35) without your seeing any blood loss. Hollow abdominal organs, such as the intestines, can rupture and drain their contents into the abdominal and pelvic cavities, producing a painful and serious inflammatory reaction and infection. The victim can go into shock from severe infection.

Abdominal Organ	Location
Liver	RUQ
Stomach	LUQ
Duodenum	Mid-upper quadrant above the belly button
Spleen	LUQ
Pancreas	LUQ
Small and large intestine	All quadrants
Bladder and Uterus	Mid-lower quadrant below the belly button
Kidneys	Right and left sides of upper back, under ribcage

RUQ = right upper quadrant
LUQ = left upper quadrant
RLQ = right lower quadrant
LLQ = left lower quadrant (see fig. 21).

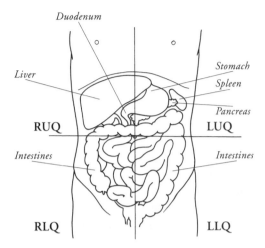

Duodenum

Liver

Stomach

Spleen

Pancreas

RUQ   LUQ

Intestines   *Intestines*

RLQ   LLQ

Figure 21. Location of abdominal organs by quadrant.

☀ WHEN TO WORRY
Penetrating Injuries (Gunshot and Stab Wounds)

Penetrating injuries to the abdomen are puncture wounds produced by sharp objects like a knife, or by a projectile such as a bullet or arrow. It is difficult in the backcountry to determine whether or not the object has punctured all the way through the skin and fat and produced an injury to the internal organs. **Therefore always assume the worst, and evacuate the victim as soon as possible to a medical facility.**

SIGNS AND SYMPTOMS

- Look for a hole in the skin (a portion of the intestines may be protruding through it).
- The victim will have abdominal pain and with internal organ injury he will be unable to relax the muscles in his abdomen.

TREATMENT

1. Anticipate and treat for shock (see p. 33).
2. Do not push any protruding intestine back into the abdominal cavity. Instead cover it with sterile 4 by 4 inch gauze dressings that are kept moist with disinfected water or sterile saline solution at all times. Place several more layers of dry dressings or a towel over the wound to minimize heat loss.
3. Leave any penetrating object in place and stabilize it with bulky dressings, clothing, and tape.

☀️ Blunt Abdominal Injuries (Blows to the Abdomen)

A blow to the abdomen can result in internal injury to the internal organs of the abdomen and bleeding, even though nothing penetrates the skin. Examine the abdomen by pressing on it gently with the tips of your fingers sequentially in all four quadrants. Push slowly and observe for pain, muscle spasms or rigidity. Normal abdomens are soft and not tender when pressed.

SIGNS AND SYMPTOMS

The following signs and symptoms may indicate internal abdominal injuries:

- Signs of shock (see p. 35).
- Pain in the abdomen that is at first mild and then becomes severe.
- Distention (bloating) of the abdomen.
- Pain or rigidity (tightness or hardness) of the belly muscles when you press in on the abdomen. (The victim may be unable to relax the muscles in his abdomen.)
- Pain referred to the left or right shoulder tip may indicate a ruptured spleen.
- Nausea or vomiting.
- Bloody urination.
- Pain in the abdomen that is made significantly worse with any movement.
- Fever.

TREATMENT

1. Anticipate and treat for shock (see p. 35).
2. Do not allow the victim to eat or drink.
3. Immediately evacuate the victim to a medical facility (see Appendix C).

CHAPTER 10

Spine Injuries

FRACTURES OF THE NECK AND BACK can damage the spinal cord and lead to permanent paralysis. Any accident that places excessive force or pressure on the head, neck, or back—such as a fall, diving accident, or head injury—can also result in a fracture of the spine. The spinal column is made up of rectangular bones, called vertebrae, that encase and protect the delicate spinal cord. The spinal cord extends from the brain to the lower back and is made up of nerves that carry messages to and from all parts of the body. If the spinal cord is crushed or severed, the parts of the body supplied by the nerves below the injury are cut off from the brain, resulting in paralysis and loss of sensation from the point of injury down.

The decision to initiate and to maintain immobilization of the spine in the wilderness has more significant ramifications than it does in the urban environment, where emergency departments are close by. An otherwise walking victim who could participate in his own evacuation would require a potentially expensive and arduous rescue if his spine were immobilized. The added delay could worsen other injuries and predispose the victim and the rest of the party to hypothermia (see p. 164) or other environmental hazards. Although in general it is always better to err on the side of being overprotective, everyone with a bump or cut on their head does not need to have their spine immobilized.

☀ WHEN TO WORRY
Potential Spine Injury

If a victim has any *one* of the following signs or symptoms after trauma, suspect a spinal injury and immobilize the spine (see p. 68).

SIGNS AND SYMPTOMS

- The victim is unconscious.
- Numbness, tingling, or diminished sensation in any part of an arm or leg.

- The victim feels pain in the back of the neck or in the middle of the back, or experiences a sharp pain when those areas are touched.
- Weakness or inability to move the arms, legs, hands, or feet.
- After sustaining a possible spine injury the victim has an altered level of consciousness or he acts like he is under the influence of drugs or alcohol.
- A victim who has suffered trauma to his head, neck, or back has another very painful injury that may distract him from appreciating the pain in his neck, such as a femur (thigh bone) or pelvic fracture, dislocated shoulder, or a broken rib.

TREATMENT

1. If a spine injury is suspected, the rescuer should immobilize the victim's head, neck, and trunk to prevent any movement of the torso. If the victim is lying in a dangerous location and must be moved quickly, the victim's head and neck should be held firmly by one rescuer's hands, while as many people as available place their arms under the victim from either side. The rescuer at the head says: "Ready, go," and with everyone lifting simultaneously, the victim is lifted as a unit and moved to a safer location. After the victim is moved, one rescuer should remain at his head and continue to hold the head and neck firmly until the spine is adequately immobilized.
2. If the neck lies at an angle to the body, one rescuer should pull the head away from the neck (very gently) while straightening it. A second rescuer should then place a cervical collar around the neck to provide some support (see below).
3. Cervical collars alone do not provide adequate immobilization of the spine. After putting a collar around the neck, fill plastic bags, stuff sacks, or socks with sand or dirt and place them on either side of the head and neck to stabilize it. Rolled-up towels, clothing, or sleeping pads are also good for this purpose. Secure these side supports to the head with tape or straps to prevent any side-to-side movement.
4. If the victim must be rolled or turned to place insulation or a spine board under him (see below), or if he is vomiting, logroll him (see fig. 1) with the head and body maintained as a straight unit.
5. In the event of a suspected spinal injury, it is generally better to send for professional rescue assistance rather than attempt to transport the victim yourself. If you must transport the victim yourself, logroll him onto a firm, flat board prior to transport.

Backcountry Tricks
Improvising a Cervical Collar

A cervical collar can be improvised by using a SAM® splint, sleeping pad, newspaper, backpack hipbelt, fanny pack, life jacket, or clothing.

SAM® Splint Cervical Collar. Create a bend in the SAM® splint approximately 6 inches from the end of the splint. This bend will form the front support that holds the chin.

Place the front support underneath the chin and wrap the remainder of the splint around the neck (fig. 22A). Create side supports by squeezing the slack in the splint together to form flares under each ear (fig. 22B). Finally, squeeze the back of the splint in a similar manner to create a back support and secure the whole thing with tape.

Sleeping Pad Collar. Fold a sleeping pad longways into thirds and center it over the back of the victim's neck. Wrap the pad around the neck, under the chin, and secure it in place with tape (fig. 23). If the pad is not long enough, extensions can be taped or tied on. Blankets, beach towels, or even a rolled plastic tarp can be used in a similar fashion.

Padded Hipbelt. A padded hipbelt taken from a large internal- or external-frame backpack can sometimes be modified, after removal, to function as a cervical collar. If the belt is too long, overlap the ends and secure them with duct tape.

Clothing. Any bulky item of clothing can be used to fashion a cervical collar. Wrap a wide elastic (Ace®) bandage around the entire item first, to compress the material and to make it more rigid and supportive before placing it on the neck.

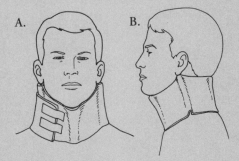
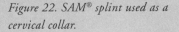

Figure 22. SAM® splint used as a cervical collar.

Figure 23. Sleeping pad used as a cervical collar.

💡 Backcountry Tricks
Improvising a Spine Board

Internal-Frame Pack/Snow Shovel System. Many internal-frame backpacks can easily be modified into a spine board by inserting a snow shovel through the center of the pack and securing it with tape (the shovel handgrip may need to be removed first). The victim's head is taped to the lightly padded shovel, which serves as a head bed (fig. 24). The remainder of the pack suspension system secures the shoulder and torso of the victim as if he were wearing the pack.

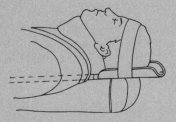

Figure 24. Head and neck immobilized using an internal-frame pack and a snow shovel.

Inverted-Pack System. A short spine board can be made using an inverted internal- or external-frame backpack. The padded lumbar pad is used as a head bed, and the hipbelt secures the pack to the victim's forehead. The pack frame is used as a short board in conjunction with an improvised cervical collar (fig. 25).

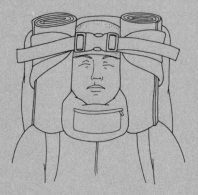

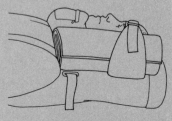

Figure 25. Inverted pack system for head and neck immobilization.

Kayak/Canoe Pillars. A makeshift backboard can be improvised from the minicell, ethafoam, or plastic pillars used to support the deck of a kayak or canoe. A plastic kayak can even be cut in half with a very sharp knife to make a firm platform to carry a victim.

CHAPTER 11

Back Pain

NEXT TO THE COMMON COLD, BACK PAIN is the nation's most common medical complaint. It ranks among the top ten most common ailments in backpackers. The lower part of the back, the lumbar spine, holds most of the weight of the body and therefore is most likely to give problems.

PREVENTION

Preventing a back injury is a whole lot easier than trying to recover from one. While on the trail, there are several things you can do to lessen the chances of injuring your back:

- Stretch before lifting your pack, especially in the morning when your muscles are cold and stiff.
- When putting on a heavy pack, keep your back straight and in a neutral position. Slide your pack onto one thigh and slip one shoulder into a loosened shoulder strap. Roll the pack onto your back and use your legs, not your back and arms, to lift yourself up.
- When lifting, always keep objects close to the body.
- Adjust the pack so as much weight as possible is on the hipbelt, instead of on the shoulder straps.
- Use a walking stick for added balance and support.

●⁂WHEN TO WORRY
Severe Back Pain

If back pain is severe and not made worse with movement or change in position, it may be due to a serious internal abdominal problem, which can cause the pain to radiate to the back. The victim should be evacuated to a medical facility as soon as possible (see Appendix C).

The victim should *also* be evacuated to a medical facility as soon as possible if he experiences *any* of the following symptoms:
- Loss of sensation in one or both of the legs or feet.
- Interference with bowel or bladder function.
- Weakness in a leg or foot.

Muscle Strain

The most common cause of back pain in the backcountry is strained muscles from overexertion or lifting heavy objects. Muscle strains in the back can range from producing mild pain to pain that is so severe, the victim is unable to sit up.

SIGNS AND SYMPTOMS
- Pain in the back that is worsened by movement (such as bending over) and made better by lying on a flat surface with the legs elevated on pillows placed under the knees.
- Pushing on the painful area usually increases the pain.

TREATMENT
1. If possible, have the victim rest on his back with a pillow under his knees, or on his side with a pillow between his legs, for 1 to 2 days before resuming gentle and graded activity. Extended bedrest beyond 2 days is not recommended because it can actually weaken the back more and slow recovery. Most people with a strained back will recover on their own within 2 to 4 weeks.
2. Nonsteroidal anti-inflammatory medications such as ibuprofen (Advil® or Motrin®) (600 mg taken three times a day with meals for 5 to 7 days) may help relieve pain and speed healing.
3. Application of cold compresses will decrease pain and swelling.

Herniated (Ruptured) Disc

Intervertebral discs are situated between the vertebral bones in the neck and back and provide shock absorption. When placed under stress, they can rupture and extrude out into the nerve canal resulting in nerve impingement. The most common location for a disc to rupture is in the lower back. Rupture can occur with heavy lifting or even after a simple sneeze.

SIGNS AND SYMPTOMS
- Pain typically radiates into the buttock and thigh region and may extend down one of the legs (sciatica). The pain is made worse in the leg when the leg is kept straight and lifted upward (straight-leg-raise test).
- The pain felt in the leg or buttock is often worse than the pain in the back.

- The pain increases with sitting and leaning forward, coughing, sneezing, and straining, and improves with lying.
- Numbness, tingling or loss of sensation may occur in the leg or foot on the side of the herniation.
- The victim may lose control over his bowel or bladder function.

TREATMENT
1. Treatment is the same as for back muscle strain.
2. The victim should be evacuated to a medical center as soon as possible (see Appendix C).

Kidney Stones

Kidney stones are hard deposits that develop in the urinary tract and produce extreme pain felt predominantly in the back. They range in size from a grain of sand to a golf ball. Kidney stones are three times more common in men than in women and typically develop during middle age. Other predisposing factors are dehydration and a diet high in protein or calcium.

Most kidney stones will eventually pass on their own. Some require surgical removal. Occasionally kidney stones can lead to infection and damage of the kidney.

SIGNS AND SYMPTOMS
- Sudden onset of very severe pain, usually starting in the flank area or back and later radiating to the groin.
- The victim typically rolls from side to side in an effort to find a more comfortable position.
- Nausea and vomiting.
- Urge to urinate.
- Blood in the urine.

TREATMENT
1. Drinking plenty of fluids—at least 4 liters a day—may help flush out the kidney stone and prevent new ones from forming.
2. Administer pain medication. Ibuprofen (Motrin®, Advil®) 800 mg every 8 hours with food is excellent for kidney stone pain, as are other nonsteroidal anti-inflammatory drugs such as naproxen (Aleve®, Naprosyn®)— see Appendix B.

Kidney Infections

A kidney infection (pyelonephritis) (see p. 198) will often produce back pain and can be mistaken for a back injury. See Chapter 28 for information on diagnosing and treating a kidney infection.

CHAPTER 12

Fractures

A FRACTURE IS ANY BREAK OR CRACK IN a bone. An *open fracture*—also called a compound fracture—is one in which the overlying skin at the fracture site has been punctured or cut, either by sharp bone ends protruding through the skin or by a direct blow that breaks the skin as it fractures the bone. The bone may or may not be visible in the wound. A closed fracture is one in which there is no wound on the skin anywhere near the fracture site. A *closed fracture* can become an open fracture if it is not handled carefully.

Open fractures are more likely to produce significant blood loss than closed ones. The bone is also contaminated by being exposed to the outside environment and may become infected. An infection in the bone is very difficult to treat and may cause long-term problems.

GENERAL GUIDELINES

It may be difficult to differentiate a fractured bone from a sprained ligament (see p. 104) or bruised muscle. When in doubt, splint the extremity (see below) and assume it is fractured until you can obtain an x-ray.

GENERAL SIGNS AND SYMPTOMS OF FRACTURES

- Deformity of a limb: compare the injured limb with the uninjured one; look for differences in length, rotation, angulation, or abnormal prominences.
- Pain and tenderness over a specific point.
- Inability to use the extremity: for example, someone who twists an ankle and is unable to bear weight should be suspected of having a broken ankle rather than a sprained ankle.
- Rapid swelling and bruising (black and blue discoloration).
- Crepitus (grating): a grinding sensation can sometimes be felt and heard when a fractured limb is touched or moved.
- Abnormal motion: motion at a point in a limb where no joint exists indicates a fracture.

Backcountry Tricks
Diagnosing a Fracture by Sound

> Sound is conducted down a broken bone more weakly than in a bone that is intact. If you have a stethoscope, you can listen over one end of a bone while tapping over the other end of the same bone. A marked difference in the sound heard in the injured bone (the sound will be dampened) compared with the sound heard in the corresponding noninjured bone on the other side of the body may indicate a fracture.

GENERAL TREATMENT GUIDELINES

There are certain guidelines to follow, regardless of which bone is fractured. Generally the goal is to minimize bleeding and further damage to bone, muscle, nerves, and blood vessels, reduce pain and suffering, and facilitate transport of the victim to a medical facility.

1. Instead of removing the victim's clothing, cut away the clothing at the fracture site with blunt-tipped bandage scissors. Cutting away just a portion of clothing minimizes movement of the victim and leaves him better protected from the environment than if whole items of clothing are removed.

2. Inspect the site of injury for any deformity, angulation, or damage to the skin.

3. Stop any bleeding with direct pressure (see p. 24).

4. Check the circulation below or downstream of the fracture site by feeling for pulses and inspecting the skin for abnormal color changes. Paleness or bluish discoloration, or a colder hand or foot compared with the noninjured side, may indicate an injured blood vessel. Without circulation, a limb can only survive for about 6 to 8 hours.

5. Check sensation on the limb by pricking the skin with a safety pin to determine if the sharp sensation is felt equally on both the injured limb and the corresponding noninjured limb on the opposite side. A difference indicates damage to a nerve.

6. Splint all fractures (see p. 77–78) before the victim is moved unless his life is in immediate danger. Splinting decreases movement of the broken bones, reduces pain, and prevents further injury to muscles, nerves, and blood vessels. It also makes it easier to evacuate the victim.

7. In general, straightening a fractured limb is not advised, unless circulation to the extremity seems impaired or gross deformity prevents splinting and

transportation. If the limb must be realigned, it is easier to do immediately, before swelling and pain make the process more difficult.

8. Administer pain medication (see Appendix B).

9. All victims with a suspected fracture should be evacuated to a medical facility as soon as possible.

Realigning a Closed Fracture. If the limb is markedly deformed and circulation to the extremities seems impaired, consider realigning or straightening the fractured limb.

1. Pull gently on the limb below the fracture site in a direction that straightens the limb while someone else holds countertraction on the limb above the fracture site (fig. 26). (Countertraction is performed by two people: one holds the upper part of the victim's limb and keeps it from moving while the other pulls the limb downstream.) Discontinue the maneuver if the victim complains of a dramatic increase in pain.

2. After the limb has been straightened, continue to hold traction while applying a splint (see below). If you cannot realign the fracture, splint the limb as it lies.

3. After any manipulation, recheck to see whether circulation has been restored or improved (see General Treatment Guidelines, above).

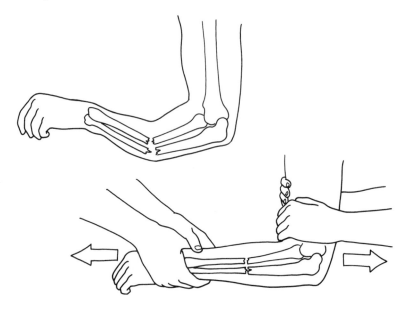

Figure 26. Realigning a deformed fracture.

Treatment of Open Fractures. Open fractures require two additional procedures.

1. Rinse or irrigate the wound with sterile saline solution or disinfected water to remove any obvious dirt and then cover it with a sterile dressing.
2. Do not try to realign the bone or push the bone back under the skin unless it is necessary for splinting and evacuation, or if there are signs of diminished circulation, such as coldness, paleness, or blue discoloration of the extremity.

Realigning an Open Fracture. If the limb is markedly deformed and circulation to the extremities seems impaired, consider realigning or straightening the fractured limb.

1. Clean any visible bone with sterile saline solution or disinfected water, using forceful irrigation (see p. 114).
2. Pull gently on the limb below the fracture site in a direction that straightens the limb while someone else holds countertraction on the same limb above the fracture site (countertraction is performed by two people: one holds the upper part of the victim's limb and keeps it from moving while the other pulls the limb downstream). Continue until the limb is realigned.
3. While continuing to hold traction, immediately splint the limb (see below) to prevent further motion and damage.
4. Cover the wound with a sterile dressing and bandage.

Splinting. In general, a splint should be rigid and well-padded, and long enough to include the joint above and below the fracture. Ideally, a splint should immobilize the fractured bone and corresponding joint in a position of function. Functional position for the various joints are as follows:

Knee: leg almost straight, with a slight flexion at the knee (place a rolled-up towel behind the knee).
Ankle: ankle and elbow bent at 90 degrees.
Wrist: wrist straight or slightly extended.
Fingers: fingers flexed in a curve as if one were attempting to hold a can of soda or a baseball.

1. Remove all constrictive jewelry such as watches, bracelets, and rings before applying the splint.
2. Use plenty of padding, especially at the bony prominences of the wrist, elbow, ankle, and knees.
3. If possible, fashion the splint on the uninjured body part on the other side of the body and then transfer it to the injured area to minimize pain.
4. Secure the splint in place with strips of clothing, belts, pieces of rope, webbing, pack straps, elastic bandages, or gauze bandages.

5. Elevate the injured body part as much as possible after splinting to minimize swelling.
6. Always check the pulse and circulation (see p. 26) after applying a splint or doing any manipulation. Check the limb often to make certain that swelling inside the splint has not cut off the circulation.
7. Administer pain medication (see Appendix B).

Jaw Fractures

Fracture of the jaw bone (mandible) occurs from direct impact with a hard object. The jaw bone usually breaks near the angle of the lower jaw, under the ear. There is often associated dental trauma.

SIGNS AND SYMPTOMS
- Pain and swelling at the site.
- Inability to open or close the mouth normally.
- Teeth do not fit together in a normal fashion when the mouth is closed.
- Bleeding around the teeth.

TREATMENT
1. Follow General Treatment Guidelines for fractures (see above).
2. Apply ice to the site to reduce swelling and pain.
3. Immobilize the jaw by wrapping and tying an elastic wrap under the chin, up the side of the face, around the top of the head, and back down the other side of the face to the chin.
4. Administer oral antibiotics such as penicillin 500 mg every 4 hours if available (see Appendix B).
5. The victim should be restricted to a liquid diet.

Facial Fractures

Fractures of the nose and cheek bones are the most common fractures of the face. These occur from direct blows to the face and can be associated with other head injuries such as a concussion of the brain, eye or dental injuries.

SIGNS AND SYMPTOMS
- The victim's cheekbones or the bones around the eyes are tender when touched.
- The cheek may appear flat or depressed.
- Swelling and black-and-blue discoloration of the skin.
- Grasp the upper teeth between your thumb and forefinger and gently rock the teeth back and forth. Abnormal movement of the upper face when you do this indicates a facial fracture.
- The victim may have double vision, especially when he looks upward.
- The fractured side of the face may feel numb.
- There may be bleeding from the nose.

TREATMENT
1. Elevate the victim's head and apply ice to reduce swelling.
2. See treatment for nosebleeds (p. 53).
3. Administer pain medication (see Appendix B).
4. Monitor the victim for signs of an obstructed airway (see p. 16).

Collarbone (Clavicle) Fractures

Collarbone fractures are most frequently caused by a fall directly onto the shoulder. Eighty percent of all collarbone fractures occur in the middle part of the clavicle. Although pain can be severe, complications and permanent disability are rare.

SIGNS AND SYMPTOMS
- The victim will usually hold his arm against the chest wall for support and to prevent motion of the broken bone.
- The collarbone will be tender to touching, and there may be a lump or swelling at the site.

TREATMENT
1. Follow General Treatment Guidelines for fractures (see p. 75).
2. Splint the victim's arm (the one on the same side as the collarbone) against the chest with a sling and swathe or safety pin sling (see below). The elbow should not be flexed past 90 degrees to avoid pinching off any blood vessels around the elbow.
3. Administer pain medication (see Appendix B).

The Sling and Swathe

A **sling** is a triangular bandage that supports the shoulder and arm. A **swathe** is another triangular bandage folded to about a 4-inch width that secures the slinged arm tightly to the chest.

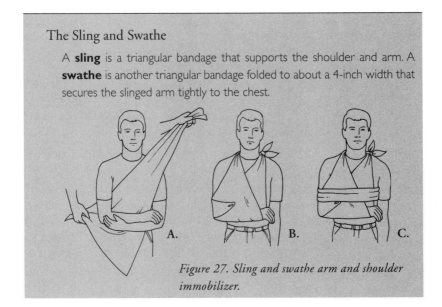

Figure 27. Sling and swathe arm and shoulder immobilizer.

To apply a sling, place a triangular bandage between the injured arm and the chest wall, with the point extending beyond the elbow of the injured arm and the long end draped over the opposite shoulder (A). Take the bottom end of the triangle bandage and bring it up and over the victim's arm and shoulder on the injured side. Pull up on the ends so that the arm rests at 90 degrees and tie the ends with a square knot (B).

To apply a swathe, wrap a triangular bandage folded to a width of about 4 inches around the injured arm and torso, halfway between the elbow and shoulder. Tie the two ends with a square knot (C).

💡 Backcountry Tricks
Improvising a Sling with Safety Pins

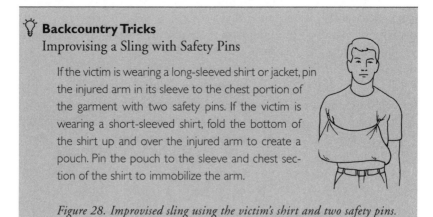

If the victim is wearing a long-sleeved shirt or jacket, pin the injured arm in its sleeve to the chest portion of the garment with two safety pins. If the victim is wearing a short-sleeved shirt, fold the bottom of the shirt up and over the injured arm to create a pouch. Pin the pouch to the sleeve and chest section of the shirt to immobilize the arm.

Figure 28. Improvised sling using the victim's shirt and two safety pins.

Shoulder and Upper Arm (Humerus) Fractures

Most fractures to the shoulder and upper arm result from a fall directly onto those areas. Sometimes an upper arm fracture can occur indirectly when a victim falls on an outstretched hand with the elbow extended. The force is transmitted up the arm causing a bone in the upper arm or shoulder to break. Fractures to the shoulder and arm can also produce nerve and blood vessel damage. The nerve most often injured with an upper arm fracture is the radial nerve, which leads to wrist drop (inability of the victim to extend the wrist).

SIGNS AND SYMPTOMS
- The site of the fracture is tender and painful when touched.
- The site of the fracture shows deformity, and the victim cannot use his arm.
- Victims with a fractured arm should still be able to bring the injured arm in tightly against the chest and be able to touch the opposite shoulder with the

hand of the injured arm. If he cannot do this suspect a shoulder dislocation (see p. 94).

TREATMENT

1. Follow General Treatment Guidelines for fractures (see p. 75).
2. Upper-arm fractures should be immobilized with a well-padded splint that extends from the armpit down the inner part of the arm, around the elbow, and back up the outside of the arm to the shoulder (fig. 29).
3. After splinting, secure the arm against the body using a sling and swathe or a safety pin sling (see figs. 27 and 28). The elbow should not be flexed past 90 degrees to avoid pinching off any blood vessels around the elbow.

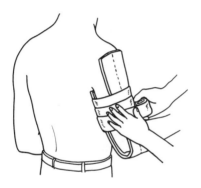

Figure 29. Splint for upper arm (humerus) fracture.

Elbow, Forearm, and Wrist Fractures

Elbow, forearm, and wrist fractures usually are caused by a fall on an out-stretched hand.

SIGNS AND SYMPTOMS

- A broken wrist sometimes has a deformity which makes it look like an upside-down fork.
- Pain and swelling at the site of the fracture.
- Pain with movement.

TREATMENT

1. Follow General Treatment Guidelines for fractures (see p. 75).
2. If there is an obvious deformity, and circulation has been compromised to the hand (there is no pulse at the wrist, and the hand is turning blue and cold compared with the uninjured hand), apply firm traction (see p. 78) to straighten the deformity.
3. A splint for a wrist, forearm, or elbow fracture should include both the elbow and hand. Apply a well-padded, U-shaped splint that extends from the hand to the elbow on both sides and wraps around the elbow like a sandwich (fig. 30).

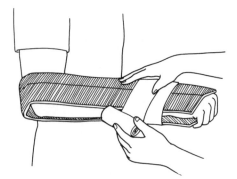

Figure 30. U-shaped splint for elbow, forearm, or wrist injuries.

The elbow should be bent at 90 degrees and the wrist should be as straight as possible, with the fingers curled around the end of the splint.

4. After splinting, secure the arm against the body using a sling and swathe or a safety pin sling (see figs. 27 and 28).

Hand and Finger Fractures

Fractures of the hand and fingers usually result from bending of the bone, such as when someone gets their finger pulled back or when a closed fist is driven into a solid object. Fractures can also occur from a direct blow to the hand or from impingement of the bone between two hard objects.

SIGNS AND SYMPTOMS
- Pain and swelling at the site of the fracture.
- If the fracture is displaced, there may be a noticeable deformity at the site of the fracture.

TREATMENT
1. Follow General Treatment Guidelines for fractures (see p. 75).
2. Remove any jewelry from the hand.
3. For a fractured hand, place a rolled pair of socks or elastic bandage in the palm to keep the fingers curled in a grabbing position (position of function) (fig. 31). Splint the arm and curled hand in place with a flat, firm object and

Figure 31. Splint for hand or wrist injuries.

an elastic or gauze bandage. Keep the tips of the fingers uncovered in order to check circulation.

4. Splint a broken finger by taping the injured finger to an adjacent uninjured finger (buddy-taping). Place some cotton or gauze between the fingers to prevent chafing (fig. 32).

5. Elevate hand injuries to minimize swelling (by using a sling or propping the hand up on some pillows).

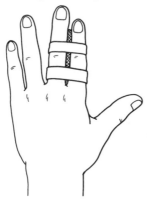

Figure 32. Buddy-taping a broken finger.

Rib Fractures

For general information and signs and symptoms, see "Broken Ribs," p. 59.

💣 Pelvic Fractures

Fractures of the pelvis are a serious injury and are often associated with other major internal injuries, such as damage to the bladder or intestines, and internal bleeding. The victim can go into shock (see p. 35) and even bleed to death internally.

SIGNS AND SYMPTOMS

• The victim may feel pain in the pelvis, hip, or lower back. Pain can also radiate down to the knee on the involved side. Pressing gently on the pelvis at the beltline will produce pain.

• The victim is unable to stand.

• If the bladder or urethra is damaged, there may be blood in the urine, or the victim may be unable to urinate. (Males may show blood at the tip of the penis.)

TREATMENT

1. Follow General Treatment Guidelines for fractures (see p. 75).

2. Place padding between the victim's legs and gently tie the legs together

to stabilize the fracture in a position that is most comfortable for the victim.

3. Treat for shock (see p. 35), but do *not* elevate the legs.
4. Evacuate the victim immediately to a medical facility. Keep him on a well-padded but firm surface during evacuation (see Appendix C).

💣 Thigh Bone (Femur) Fractures

The femur is the largest bone in the body, and it takes a great amount of force for it to break. There may be associated injury to muscles, nerves, and blood vessels. When the femur breaks, the thigh muscles go into spasm, pulling the thigh into a more spherical shape (resulting in a greater amount of space for blood to escape into the surrounding tissues). Massive bleeding can occur and the patient can go into shock and die without losing any visible blood externally. The broken bone ends will overlap and dig into the muscle, causing additional injury, extreme pain, and further internal blood loss.

SIGNS AND SYMPTOMS

- There is extreme pain at the fracture site. Swelling may be apparent or not noticeable.
- If the femur is fractured at the mid point, the leg will appear shortened and the foot will be rotated outward away from the other leg. If the fracture is very close to the hip, the leg may be rotated, but not appear significantly shortened.
- Circulation to the foot may be impaired. The foot may be cold and you may be unable to detect a pulse on top of the foot.
- Shock may occur (see p. 35).
- Crepitus or grating may sometimes be felt at the fracture site.

TREATMENT

The best splint for a femur fracture is one that produces traction to stretch the muscles back to their normal length. A traction splint will significantly reduce blood loss, muscle spasms, and pain, and will facilitate evacuation.

1. Follow General Treatment Guidelines for fractures (see p. 75).
2. Apply traction with your hands by holding the victim's foot and pulling the leg back into normal alignment. If there are multiple rescuers, pull the injured leg out to its normal length, using the uninjured leg as a guide. Once you have started pulling traction, *do not* release it. If you are alone with the victim, create a traction splint first, then pull and maintain traction with the device.
3. Evacuate the victim immediately to a medical facility (see Appendix C).

Backcountry Tricks
Improvising a Traction Splint for a Broken Femur

A traction splint is a device that provides stability and support to the fractured femur and keeps the broken bone segments from overriding each other. It helps to reduce pain and muscle spasms, and limits bleeding into the tissues.

There are a variety of techniques for improvising a traction splint with limited materials in the backcountry. An improvised traction splint has six components:

1. Ankle hitch (for pulling traction on the leg).
2. Upper thigh (crotch) hitch (for providing countertraction to the leg).
3. Rigid support that is longer than the leg.
4. Method for securing the two hitches to the rigid support.
5. Method for producing traction (trucker's hitch).
6. Padding.

Warning: Before applying an improvised splint to the victim, test your creation on a noninjured member of your party, or at least on the noninjured leg of the victim.

1. **Apply an ankle hitch.** This will be used to pull traction on the leg. It is a stirrup tied around the foot and ankle, or the lower calf. There are three different techniques that can be used to make an ankle hitch. It is best to leave the shoe on the victim's foot and apply the hitch over it. Cut out the toe section of the shoe to periodically check the circulation (see p. 26) in the foot.

   Double runner system

   i. Fold two long (5 feet), narrow (1 ½ to 2 inches), and strong pieces of material in half to create loops. Ideal materials include webbing, triangular bandages or bandannas folded lengthwise and tied together, pieces of thick rope, or even well-padded shoelaces.

   ii. Lay one loop over and one loop behind the ankle, making sure the open ends of each loop are facing in opposite directions (fig. 33A).

   iii. Pull the ends of the material through the loops on both sides. The hitch should fit snugly and flat against the ankle.

   iv. Adjust the two pieces of material so the ends are centered under the arch of the shoe and the traction is in line with the leg (fig. 33B). The foot should be at a 90-degree angle to the ankle.

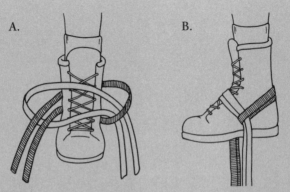

Figure 33A-B. Double runner system ankle hitch for traction splinting.

S-configuration hitch. The S-configuration hitch is preferred if the victim also has an injury to the foot or ankle, because traction is pulled from the victim's calf instead of his ankle.

    i. Lay an 8-inch or longer piece of webbing or other similar material over the front of the lower calf in an S-shaped configuration (fig. 34A).

    ii. Wrap both ends of the material behind the ankle and up through the loop on the other side (fig. 34B).

    iii. Pull the ends down on either side of the arch of the foot to tighten the hitch and tie an overhand knot (fig. 34C).

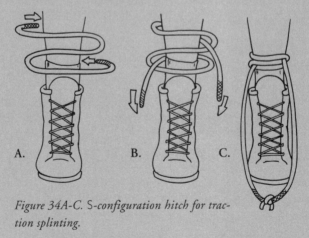

Figure 34A-C. S-configuration hitch for traction splinting.

Buck's traction. Buck's traction is more comfortable for extended transports because it greatly increases the surface area over which traction is applied and decreases the potential for painful pressure points and compression of blood vessels in the foot.

    i. Attach duct tape to a folded piece of sleeping pad to create a stirrup hanging loose below the fold of the pad (fig. 35A).

    ii. Secure the entire unit to the lower leg with an elastic or other improvised bandage (fig. 35B).

    iii. Check the traction periodically for slippage during transport.

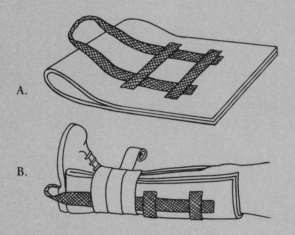

A.

B.

Figure 35A-B. Buck's traction hitch for traction splinting.

2. **Apply an upper thigh hitch.** This hitch provides an anchor for countertraction and should be placed as high up on the thigh as possible. Tightly wrap a rolled-up jacket or other material (belt, webbing, fanny pack, or pack straps) around the upper part of the thigh and tie an overhand knot (fig. 36). Climbers can use a climbing harness; paddlers can use an inverted life jacket worn like a diaper. Regardless of the material used, make sure to pad the crotch and inner thigh.

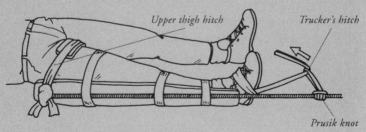

Upper thigh hitch   Trucker's hitch

Prusik knot

Figure 36. Completed improvised traction splint.

3. **Apply a rigid support to the outside of the injured leg and attach the support to the upper thigh hitch.** Place a rigid, straight object that is at least a foot longer than the leg against the outside of the leg and secure it to the upper thigh hitch with tape or strapping material (fig. 36). You can use a walking stick, one or two ski poles lashed together with duct tape, a ski, tent poles, a canoe or kayak paddle, or a straight tree branch.

4. **Attach the ankle hitch to the rigid support.** Pass the ankle hitch through an anchor point on the rigid support. An anchor point can be created by using a prusik knot (fig. 37) or, if the support is a tent pole, by placing a bent tent stake in its end.

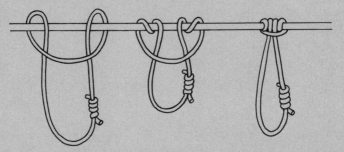

Figure 37. A prusik knot provides an anchoring or attachment point on a rigid, straight object. The knot will slide as long as it is not loaded or weighted, but will jam and hold tight if weight or tension is applied to it. A prusik knot is usually made with a loop of 5mm Kermantle rope tied at the ends. (A shoelace can be used if nothing else is available.) The loop is wrapped around the rigid object and through itself either two or three times.

5. **Apply traction.** Pull the anchor hitch back toward the foot. The amount of traction required will vary with the victim. A stopping point for pulling traction is when the injured leg appears to be back to its normal length (compare it with the uninjured leg) or when the victim is more comfortable. Use a trucker's hitch (see fig. 36) to gain mechanical advantage when pulling traction.

   After applying traction, recheck the circulation and sensation in the foot every 30 minutes. If the pulse is lost or diminished with traction, or if the foot turns blue or cold, reduce the amount of traction in the splint until the color and pulse return.

6. **Apply padding.** Pad the foot, ankle, and the leg at all points where they come into contact with the splint and hitches. Secure the entire splint firmly to the leg.

Knee Fractures

Fractures of the knee either involve the kneecap (patella), the lower end of the femur, or the upper end of the tibia or fibula. The bone most commonly fractured in the knee is the kneecap.

SIGNS AND SYMPTOMS

- A fracture of the kneecap (patella) will produce severe pain and tenderness to touching directly over the kneecap and inability to bend or straighten the knee without dramatically increasing the pain.
- Swelling around the knee.
- A fracture of the upper tibia will produce pain just below the kneecap and inability to bend or straighten the knee without dramatically increasing the pain.

TREATMENT

1. Follow General Treatment Guidelines for fractures (see p. 75).
2. Fractures around the knee should be splinted from the hip to the ankle with a cylinder splint. You can use a life jacket or rolled-up sleeping pad (fig. 38).
3. Individuals with fractures near the knee should not be allowed to walk without crutches.

Lower-Leg (Tibia and Fibula) Fractures

The tibia can fracture from a direct blow or from a twisting force to the bone, as seen in ski injuries. The principal danger associated with a tibia fracture is the development of a compartment syndrome, in which bleeding and swelling in the calf lead to increased pressure in the calf. If the pressure gets high enough, vital structures such as nerves, blood vessels, and muscle are squeezed, leading to permanent damage.

SIGNS AND SYMPTOMS

- Deformity of the limb at the fracture site.
- Crepitus (grinding sounds) when leg is moved.
- Tenderness at the fracture site.
- Immediate swelling around the fracture site.
- A victim with a tibia fracture will not be able to stand on the leg.
- Some victims with an isolated fibula fracture can still walk painfully on the injured leg.

TREATMENT

1. If necessary, apply gentle traction (see above) to straighten any deformity that exists in the leg and maintain the traction while another person applies a splint.
2. For lower leg fractures, apply a splint that encompasses the leg from the knee to the ankle. A U-shaped splint running from the inner thigh above the knee

around the bottom of the foot and up the outside of the leg back to the knee, with adequate padding, is excellent.

3. After splinting, elevate the leg to reduce swelling above the level of the heart.
4. Check the circulation and sensation (see p. 26) in the foot every 30 minutes. Numbness and tingling in the foot, severe pain produced when the rescuer moves the victim's toes, or loss of pulse are a potential sign of a compartment syndrome (see above). If any of these occur, loosen the splint, elevate the leg higher, and speed up the evacuation if possible.

💡 Backcountry Tricks
Improvising a Knee and Lower-Leg Splint

Wrap a sleeping pad around the lower leg from the mid-thigh to the foot (fig. 38). Fold the pad so that the top of the leg is not included in the splint. This provides better visualization of the extremity and leaves room for swelling.

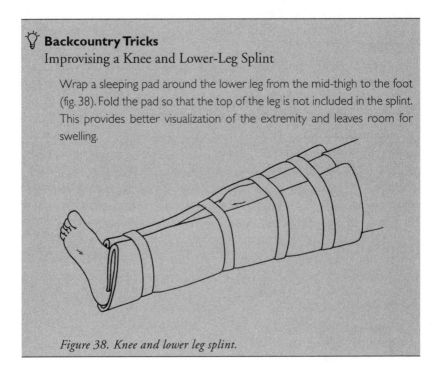

Figure 38. Knee and lower leg splint.

Ankle Fractures

The ends of the tibia and fibula overlap the smaller ankle bone (talus) slightly, producing bumps on either side of the ankle. When the ankle is twisted, the outer bump (the lateral malleolus of the fibula) sometimes cracks. This is the most common ankle fracture.

SIGNS AND SYMPTOMS

If the ankle joint swells up like a cantaloupe and is extremely painful, you should assume there's significant damage. It is hard to differentiate a broken ankle bone from a severe ligament sprain (see p. 106) in the field. Both can produce swelling, pain, and black-and-blue discoloration. Clues that the ankle is broken are:

- Inability to bear weight on the foot.
- Grinding sounds when you move the ankle around.
- Gentle pressure directly on the bump produces significant pain.
- Deformity around the ankle.

TREATMENT

1. Apply a well-padded splint that extends from halfway down the calf to the foot on both sides and wraps around the foot, encompassing the ankle like a sandwich (fig. 39). The ankle should be splinted so that the foot rests at a 90-degree angle to the leg.

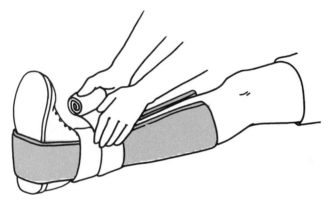

Figure 39. U-shaped splint for immobilizing an ankle fracture.

2. It is preferable to leave a loosely tied boot or shoe in place, but the tongue of the boot or shoe should be removed so that circulation (see p. 26) and sensation can be monitored.
3. Keep the foot elevated above the level of the heart as much as possible.

Foot and Toe Fractures

When the ankle is twisted, the outer bone in the foot can occasionally break instead of one of the bones in the ankle. Bones in the feet can also be fractured by direct trauma such as dropping a heavy object onto the foot. Fractures of the toes usually occur when the victim stubs or catches his toe on an obstacle.

SIGNS AND SYMPTOMS

- Swelling and pain at the fracture site.
- If the fracture is displaced, there may be a noticeable deformity.

TREATMENT

1. Following General Treatment Guidelines for fractures (see p. 75).
2. Splint a fractured toe by buddy-taping it to an adjacent toe with small pieces of tape, in the same manner as you would buddy-tape a broken finger (see fig. 32). Place some cotton or gauze material between the toes to prevent rubbing and chafing.
3. Victims with a fractured foot or toe may still be able to walk out of the backcountry under their own power with their foot supported in a protective and well-padded shoe and a walking stick.
4. If the victim is unable to stand on the foot or walk, the fractured foot should be splinted in the same manner as an ankle fracture (see above).

CHAPTER 13

Dislocations

A DISLOCATION OCCURS WHEN A BONE is pulled out of its socket at a particular joint. Dislocations often damage the supporting structures of the joint and tear the surrounding ligaments that connect the bones. Sometimes when a joint is under strain, a bone may "pop out" of position and then return spontaneously (subluxation). This will be painful, but does not require reduction (relocation or returning to normal position). A subluxation is treated as a sprain injury (see p. 104). Dislocations are most common in the shoulders, elbows, fingers, and kneecap (patella).

TO REDUCE OR NOT TO REDUCE

The reduction of a dislocation (returning the bone to its normal position) by a non-physician is controversial in wilderness medicine. Personally, I feel that there are many good reasons why a lay person should attempt to reduce a dislocation in the backcountry, especially when rapid transport to a hospital is not possible:

- Reduction is easiest soon after injury, before swelling and muscle spasm develop.
- Reduction relieves pain.
- Early reduction reduces the risk of further injury to blood vessels, nerves, and muscles. Blood vessels can become trapped, stretched, or even compressed during a dislocation, which leads to a loss of blood flow to the limb if reduction is not performed.
- It is easier to splint the extremity if the dislocation is reduced.

Even if there is a fracture in addition to the dislocation, the first step in treatment is to attempt to reduce the dislocation (although a fracture may sometimes prevent you from doing so).

GENERAL GUIDELINES

When reducing a dislocation, use steady, constant traction and avoid jerky movements. Always check the function, sensation, and circulation of any extremity before and after each reduction attempt. Check *sensation* to a limb by pricking the skin with a safety pin to determine if the sharp sensation is felt equally on both the injured limb and the corresponding noninjured limb on the opposite side. Check *circulation* by feeling for a pulse and inspecting the skin for abnormal color changes below or downstream of the injured site. Paleness or bluish discoloration, or a colder hand or foot compared with the noninjured side, may indicate a damaged blood vessel.

After a dislocation is reduced, the extremity should be splinted in the same manner as for a fracture (see Chapter 12). If a dislocation cannot be reduced, splint the extremity in the most comfortable position for the victim.

Shoulder Dislocation

Shoulder dislocations are common in kayakers and skiers because paddles and ski poles act as fulcrums, placing added force on the joint. In a shoulder dislocation, the arm is usually pulled away from the body, rotated outwards, and extended backwards. This can occur when a kayaker high-braces or attempts to roll his boat. The arm gets yanked out of its socket and lodges in front of the joint.

SIGNS AND SYMPTOMS

- Victims are usually in severe pain and aware that something is out of joint.
- The shoulder may look squared off, lacking the normal rounded contour.
- The victim will usually hold the arm on the injured side away from the body with the uninjured arm and be unable to bring it in tightly into his chest. If the victim can bring the injured arm across the body in a normal position for splinting and touch his opposite shoulder with his hand, then you should assume he does *not* have a shoulder dislocation, and not attempt reduction. He may have a muscle strain, upper-arm fracture (see p. 80), clavicle fracture (see p. 79), or shoulder separation (see below).

TREATMENT

1. Before attempting to reduce the shoulder, check the pulse in the wrist and the circulation (see above) in the hand. Check the nerve function by asking the victim to move his wrist up and down and to move all of his fingers. Test for sensation (see above). Note whether or not there is any abnormality with circulation, sensation, or function.

2. There are many good techniques for reducing a shoulder dislocation (see sidebar below). In the backcountry, the key is to do it quickly, before the muscles spasm. This is facilitated by reducing the shoulder with the victim standing or sitting, rather than hunting for a flat place to lay him down.

3. *Warning: If a dislocated shoulder cannot be reduced after two attempts, or if the reduction maneuver produces a dramatic increase in pain, the attempt should be aborted and the arm immobilized in the most comfortable*

position for the victim. This usually requires placing a pillow or rolled blanket under the armpit, between the arm and chest wall.

4. After the shoulder is reduced, recheck the victim's circulation, sensation, and ability to move his fingers and wrist. Immobilize the arm with a sling and swathe or a safety pin sling (see figs. 27 and 28).

Reducing a Dislocated Shoulder

One-Person Weiss Technique

In this technique, both the victim and the rescuer are standing.

1. Standing to the side of the victim, have him bend over at the waist while you support his chest and allow his dislocated arm to hang down toward the ground (A). Support as much of the victim's weight as possible to allow him to relax.

2. With your other hand, grab the victim's wrist and turn the arm slowly outward so that the palm faces forward.

3. Apply steady downward traction and *very slowly* bring the arm forward toward the head until the shoulder is reduced or the arm reaches the same plane as the ear (B). Avoid jerky movements. You may need to hold traction for a few minutes before the arm pops back into the shoulder socket.

4. You can usually notice a clunk and shift of the arm as it returns to the joint, combined with a sigh of relief from the victim.

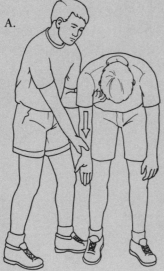

Figure 40. One-person Weiss technique for reducing a dislocated shoulder.

Two-Person Weiss Technique

In this technique, both the victim and the rescuers are standing.

1. If two rescuers are available, one should support the victim at the chest and provide countertraction while the other pulls downward on the dislocated arm in the same manner as described in number 3 above (fig. 41).

2. The person supporting the chest should also use the thumb of his other hand to push the scapula (shoulder blade) toward the backbone (inward). This scapular manipulation maneuver helps position the socket so the arm can slip back in easier.

3. You can usually notice a clunk and shift of the arm as it returns to the joint, combined with a sigh of relief from the victim.

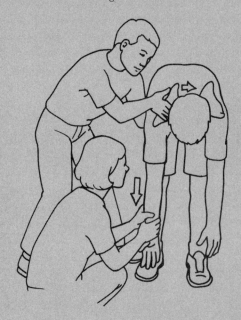

Figure 41. Two-person Weiss technique for reducing a dislocated shoulder with the victim standing.

One-Person Sitting Technique

In this technique, both the victim and the rescuer are sitting on the ground.

1. Grab the victim's forearm close to his elbow with both of your hands (fig. 42).

2. Place your foot against the victim's chest for counterbalance if necessary.

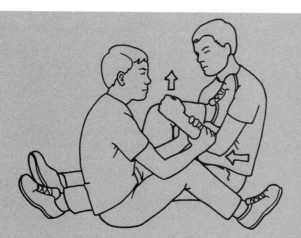

Figure 42. One-person sitting technique for reducing a dislocated shoulder.

3. With the victim's elbow bent at 90 degrees, exert steady traction on the arm by pulling his forearm away from his body.
4. After about a minute, slowly raise the entire arm upward maintaining traction, until reduction is complete. If the shoulder does not reduce with steady traction and raising the arm alone, try gingerly rotating the forearm outward while continuing to pull traction.

Two-Person Sitting Technique

In this technique, both victim and rescuers are sitting on the ground.

1. If another rescuer is available, he should provide countertraction from behind the victim while performing scapular manipulation, as described in the two-person Weiss technique (see above).
2. The rescuer in front of the victim exerts traction as described in the one-person sitting technique (see above).

Shoulder Separation

In contrast to a shoulder dislocation (in which the arm is pulled out of its socket), in a shoulder separation the acromioclavicular (AC) ligament that connects the outer part of the clavicle (collarbone) with the top of the scapula (shoulder blade) ruptures, allowing these two bones to pull apart. The AC ligament is most commonly injured when the victim falls directly onto the point of the shoulder when the arm is in close to the body. A shoulder separation can mimic and is often misdiagnosed as a collarbone fracture (see p. 79).

SIGNS AND SYMPTOMS

- Pain and swelling at the outermost part of the clavicle (collarbone).
- Pain increases with arm movement, especially if the arm is raised upward away from the side of the body.
- The outermost part of the clavicle may appear deformed. Pushing on this point will produce severe pain.
- Victims with a separated shoulder should still be able to bring the injured arm in tightly against the chest and be able to touch the opposite shoulder with the hand of the injured arm. If he cannot do this, suspect a shoulder dislocation (see above).

TREATMENT

1. Apply ice to the painful and swollen area.
2. Splint the victim's arm against the chest with a sling and swathe or a safety pin sling (see figs. 27 and 28).
3. Administer pain medication (see Appendix B).

Elbow Dislocation

Second in frequency only to shoulder dislocations, dislocations of the elbow may result from hyperextension at the elbow joint, or when a victim falls on an outstretched hand with the elbow extended.

SIGNS AND SYMPTOMS

- The dislocated elbow will appear deformed when compared with the uninjured elbow.
- There is immediate and severe pain, rapid swelling, and total loss of function of the elbow. The victim will be unable to flex (bend) or extend (straighten) the elbow.
- The arm is frequently held in flexion with the forearm appearing shorter than the forearm on the uninjured arm.
- The ulnar nerve can be damaged, leading to numbness in the ring and little fingers.

TREATMENT

Before attempting to reduce the elbow, check the pulse in the wrist, circulation in the hand, and sensation in the hand and fingers (see above). Check function by asking the victim to move his wrist up and down and to bend and straighten all of his fingers. Document any abnormality before and after attempting reduction.

Elbow dislocations require a great deal of traction and may be impossible to reduce in the backcountry. If you are unable to reduce the dislocation, immobilize the arm with a sling and swathe or a safety pin sling (see figs. 27 and 28).

1. To attempt reduction, have the victim lie on his stomach with the elbow bent at 90 degrees over the padded edge of a table or ledge (fig. 43). Pull downward and slightly outward on the wrist or forearm while another rescuer pulls upward on the upper arm. While pulling downward on the wrist, push the dislocated bony prominence at the elbow downward with your other hand.
2. After any reduction attempt, recheck the pulse in the wrist, circulation in the hand, sensation in the hand and fingers, and function of the wrist, hand, and fingers (see above).
3. After reduction, splint the elbow as though it were a fracture (see p. 81).

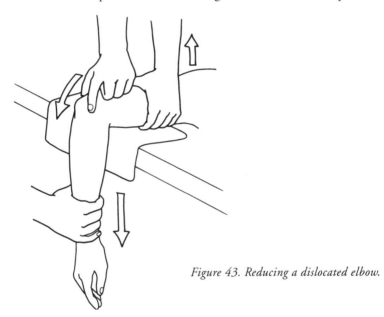

Figure 43. Reducing a dislocated elbow.

Finger Dislocation

Finger dislocations most commonly occur at the middle knuckle joint of the finger.

SIGNS AND SYMPTOMS

- The victim will be unable to move the dislocated joint.
- There will be an obvious deformity at the site of dislocation.

TREATMENT

1. Do *not* attempt to reduce a dislocation at the base of the index finger. Splint the hand in a position of comfort and seek medical attention (see p. 82 for splinting the hand for a fracture).
2. To attempt reduction of other fingers (or other joints of the index finger), pull on the tip of the finger with one hand, while pushing the base of the dislocated finger with the other hand (fig. 44).

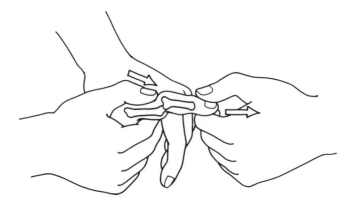

Figure 44. Reducing a dislocated finger.

3. After reduction, buddy-tape the reduced finger to an adjacent finger (see fig. 32).

💣☀ Hip Dislocation

A hip dislocation can occur when a significant and violent force is suddenly applied to the knee while it is in a flexed (bent) position. The force of impact drives the head of the femur (thigh bone) out of its joint, and in the majority of cases, the femur comes to rest behind the pelvis bone (fig. 45A).

SIGNS AND SYMPTOMS

• The victim's leg is rotated inward, and the hip and knee are both flexed (bent) (fig. 45B).

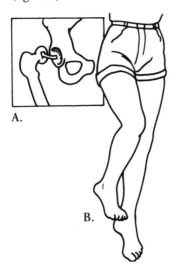

A.

B.

Figure 45A-B. Posterior hip dislocation.

- The victim will be in a great deal of pain.
- The victim cannot move or straighten the injured leg.
- The sciatic nerve may be damaged, producing numbness, tingling, and loss of sensation to the involved leg.

TREATMENT

Two people and a great deal of traction are required to reduce a pelvic hip disloca-tion. It may be impossible to accomplish in the backcountry.

1. Place the victim on his back with the knee and hip on the side of the disloca-tion both flexed at 90 degrees (fig. 46). One rescuer will hold the victim flat on the ground by pushing down with his hands on both sides of the victim's pelvic bone. The other rescuer straddles the victim's calf, locks his hands be-hind the victim's knee, and applies steady traction in an upward direction. Reducing a hip is often difficult and requires a great deal of sustained pulling to overcome the powerful leg muscles.

2. Once reduced, the injured leg on the side of the dislocation should be tied to the other leg and the victim transported to a medical facility (see Appendix C).

3. If reduction is unsuccessful, secure the leg in the most comfortable position for the victim and arrange evacuation.

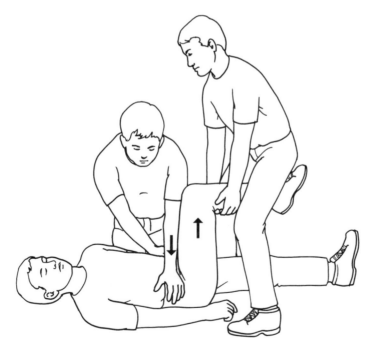

Figure 46. Reducing a dislocated hip.

Ankle Dislocation

A severely fractured ankle can also be dislocated. Fracture-dislocations of the ankle usually result from a fall onto a hard surface with the foot twisted inward or outward.

SIGNS AND SYMPTOMS

- The foot will usually be displaced inward or outward and lie at a very unnatural angle to the lower leg.
- Severe pain and swelling will be present.

TREATMENT

1. Apply gentle traction to the foot and ankle and straighten the foot until the deformity has been corrected and the ankle is better aligned.
2. Splint the ankle as you would for a fracture (see p. 90).

Patella (Kneecap) Dislocation

Dislocation of the patella usually occurs from a twisting injury while the knee is extended.

SIGNS AND SYMPTOMS

- The patella is displaced to the outer part of the knee (laterally), resulting in an obvious deformity and pain.
- The knee is usually flexed (bent) and the victim is unable to move it.

TREATMENT

1. A patella dislocation can usually be reduced quite easily by pushing the patella (kneecap) back toward the inside of the knee (medially) with your thumbs, while gently straightening the knee joint (fig. 47). The patella will pop back into place and there should be immediate relief of pain. If the maneuver is painful or not easily accomplished, do not apply excessive force.

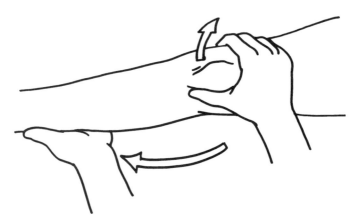

Figure 47. Reducing a dislocated patella (kneecap).

2. After the kneecap is repositioned, the victim should be able to walk with an improvised knee support, such as an ensolite pad wrapped around the knee to keep it from bending.
3. If you're unable to reduce the patella, splint the knee (see p. 89) in a position of comfort and evacuate the victim (see Appendix C).

💣 WHEN TO WORRY
Total Knee Dislocation

Do not confuse a total knee dislocation, which is a potentially catastrophic injury, with a dislocation of the patella (kneecap). A total knee dislocation may damage the popliteal artery and compromise circulation to the foot. It also results in disruption of all of the ligaments of the knee joint, causing a very loose and unstable knee joint.

SIGNS AND SYMPTOMS
• The knee is bruised and swollen and there is severe pain.
• The knee may have an obvious deformity; often it will have already reduced itself spontaneously, and not look grossly deformed.
• If the popliteal artery is damaged there may be decreased sensation and circulation to the foot (see above).

TREATMENT
1. If the knee is still out of alignment and deformed, gently reposition and straighten it by pulling on the lower leg.
2. This injury is important because very often a major artery of the leg is torn in the process. **The victim should be evacuated immediately to the nearest medical facility** (see Appendix C). If the artery is damaged it must be fixed within 6 to 8 hours to save the leg.

CHAPTER 14

Sprains and Strains

ALTHOUGH THE WORD "SPRAIN" IS typically substituted for "strain" in informal speech, the two terms describe injuries to different parts of the body. A *sprain* is the stretching or tearing of ligaments that attach one bone to another. Ligaments are sprained when a joint is twisted or stretched beyond its normal range of motion. Most sprains occur in the ankle and knee. Symptoms include tenderness at the site, swelling, bruising, and pain with movement. Since these symptoms are also present with a fracture, it may be difficult to differentiate between the two.

A *strain* is an injury to a muscle or its tendon. The tendon connects the muscle to the bone. Strains often result from overexertion, or lifting and pulling a heavy object without good body mechanics. Strains can sometimes be disabling, especially in the back. Symptoms are initially the same as for sprains.

PREVENTION

Prevent sprain and strain injuries by stretching out prior to beginning your activity. Pay attention to good body mechanics and posture while lifting or carrying heavy objects. To prevent ankle sprains, wear high-top hiking boots with good ankle support.

GENERAL TREATMENT GUIDELINES

First-aid treatment for most sprain and strain injuries is primarily damage control and can be summarized by the acronym RICES: *rest, ice, compression, elevation,* and *stabilization.*

Rest	Resting takes the stress off the injured joint and prevents further damage to ligaments and tendons.
Ice	Ice reduces swelling and eases pain. For ice or cold therapy to be effective, it must be applied early and for up to 20 minutes at least 3 to 4 times a day, followed by application of a compression wrap (see below). If a compression wrap is not

applied after ice therapy, the joint will swell as soon as the ice is removed.

Compression Compression is too often neglected in the treatment of sprain injuries. Compression wraps prevent swelling and provide some support. A compression wrap can be made by placing some padding (socks, gloves, pieces of an ensolite sleeping pad) over the sprained joint and then wrapping it with an elastic bandage. Begin the wrap at the end of the extremity and move upward. For example, with an ankle sprain, start from the toes and move up the foot and over the ankle with the wrap. The wrap should be comfortably tight. Monitor the extremity for numbness, tingling, or increased pain, which may indicate that the compression wrap is too tight and should be loosened.

Elevation Elevate the injured joint above the level of the heart as much as possible to reduce swelling.

Stabilization Tape or splint (see p. 77) the injured part to prevent further injury.

RICES should be maintained for the first 72 hours after any injury. In addition:

1. Administer a nonsteroidal anti-inflammatory medication such as ibuprofen (Motrin®), 600 mg three times a day with food to reduce both pain and inflammation.

2. As soon as possible, seek medical evaluation to determine whether x-rays are needed to make sure there is no fracture.

Rehabilitation. After about 72 hours of RICES, it's time to start the rehabilitation process, even if you're still in the backcountry. Too many people falsely believe that an idle body part heals best. The truth is, ligaments mend stronger and faster if you move them around.

1. Begin by putting the sprained joint through some type of limited range-of-motion exercise to prevent stiffness, facilitate blood flow, and reduce localized swelling.

2. Start doing balance exercises to minimize the loss of coordination that occurs after immobilization or joint injury.

Healing Time. As a rule of thumb, the time required for initial healing and recovery of different tissue types is as follows:

Muscles   6–8 weeks

Bones   6–12 weeks

Tendons and Ligaments   12–36 weeks (some ligaments may
                               take 12 months or longer to heal)

Ankle Sprain

Sprained ankles are common backcountry injuries. Most often, the ligaments on the outside of the joint are the ones injured when you roll your foot inward (invert it) while walking or jumping on an uneven surface.

SIGNS AND SYMPTOMS

- There is usually pain and swelling on the outer part of the ankle.
- The victim should still be able to bear his weight. If he cannot, you should suspect an ankle fracture (see p. 90).

TREATMENT

1. First aid begins with RICES (see p. 104).
2. If the victim cannot stand and put weight on his feet, the foot and ankle must be splinted (see p. 91) and the victim evacuated (see Appendix C).
3. If the victim can still walk, the ankle should be taped for support with an open-basket crossweave stirrup pattern (see below) to prevent further injury, and facilitate further hiking.
4. After 72 hours of RICES, the victim should begin moving the ankle through a pain-free range of motion and start exercises to improve balance and coordination. An excellent first exercise is to spell the letters of the alphabet with the foot in the air, thus putting the ankle through a complete range of motion. For further coordination and balance training, he should sit in a chair or on a log and balance his foot on a board resting on a round object such as a tennis ball.

💡 Backcountry Tricks

Crossweave Tape Support for Ankle Sprains

Taping the ankle using a crossweave pattern will provide excellent support for the ankle when walking. One- to two-inch–width cloth tape is preferable.

1. Apply an anchor strip of tape halfway around the calf about 6 inches above the "bumps" in the ankle (A, no. 1). Leave a 2-inch gap between the ends of the tape to allow room for swelling .
2. Apply an additional anchor strip at the instep of the foot (no. 2). Once again, leave a 2-inch gap between the tape ends.
3. Apply the first of three to five stirrup strips (no. 3). Begin on the inside of

the upper anchor (no. 1), and wrap a piece of tape down the inside of the leg, over the inside ankle bump, across the bottom of the foot, and up the outside part of the leg, and over the outside bump, ending at the outer part of the upper anchor.

4. Apply the first of three to five interconnecting horseshoe strips (no. 4). Start on the anchor on the inside of the foot (no. 2), and wrap below the inside ankle bump, around the heel, and below the outside bump, ending on the anchor on the outer part of the foot.

5. Repeat steps 3 and 4 (B), overlapping each piece of tape by one-half its width. Be sure to leave a 2-inch gap on the top of the foot and ankle to allow room for any swelling.

6. On both sides, secure the tape ends with two strips of tape applied perpendicular to and over the tape ends.

A.

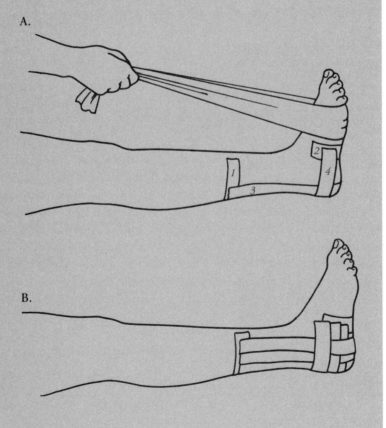

B.

Figure 48A-B. Crossweave tape support for ankle sprains.

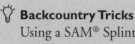
Backcountry Tricks
Using a SAM® Splint to Create an Ankle Support

A SAM® splint can stabilize a sprained ankle enough to allow the victim to walk. Wrap the SAM® splint around the foot and ankle, with the shoe in place. Secure the splint with tape. You may need to stop periodically to tighten or rewrap the splint.

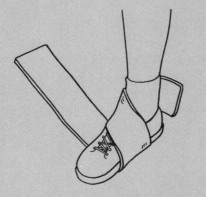

Figure 49. Wrap a SAM® splint around the ankle and shoe to provide support while walking.

Strained or Ruptured Achilles Tendon

Running or walking up a hill with a heavy load on your back can injure the Achilles tendon, which attaches your calf muscles to your heel. The tendon can even tear completely (rupture), in which case it pulls away from the bone or snaps in half.

SIGNS AND SYMPTOMS
- If the Achilles tendon is ruptured, the victim will not be able to walk or to bear his weight. He will feel as if someone stabbed the back of his ankle with a sharp object.
- If the tendon is strained but not ruptured, the victim will experience pain and discomfort with walking, but will still be able to bear his full weight and walk.

TREATMENT
1. If the tendon is strained but not completely torn, treat with RICES (see p. 104). Gently stretch the tendon to keep it flexible. The victim should gradually put weight on the foot, and then walk as the pain allows.

2. If the tendon is torn or ruptured, treat with RICES, splint the ankle (see p. 90), and evacuate the victim (see Appendix C). Surgery will be needed to repair the torn tendon.

Knee Sprains

The knee is made up of bones, ligaments, tendons, and cartilage. Like any joint, the knee is subject to overuse injuries, especially from walking up and down hills with a heavy backpack. A direct blow to the knee, as in a fall onto a rock, is most likely to produce a bruise or fracture a bone. Twisting, rotating, or falling in an awkward position is more likely to produce a sprain injury to one of the major ligaments that support the knee.

SIGNS AND SYMPTOMS

The victim of a knee sprain may note an audible crack or a pop at the time of injury, followed by immediate pain that soon turns into a dull ache. The ache may subside after a while, and the knee will swell and feel as though it is going to give way when the victim puts weight on it or turns to the side.

Knee sprains are divided into three degrees of severity based on the amount of ligament that is torn.

1. In *first-degree sprains,* there is pain, but no instability when the knee is stressed. This indicates that only a few ligament fibers are torn.
2. In *second-degree sprains,* there is pain and slight instability when the knee is stressed. This indicates that about half of the ligament fibers are torn.
3. In *third-degree sprains,* there is significant instability when moving the knee but not much pain. This indicates a completely torn ligament.

TREATMENT

1. Initial treatment of all knee sprains is RICES (see p. 104).
2. In *first-degree knee sprains,* walking can usually be resumed with little or no additional support. Treat at home with physical therapy.
3. Treatment of *second-degree knee sprains* is the same as for first-degree sprains, but recovery takes longer and surgery may eventually be required. The victim should wear a supportive knee immobilizer while walking (see fig. 50).
4. Victims with a *third-degree knee sprain* should not attempt to walk without a supportive knee immobilizer in place. Even with a third-degree tear, many victims will still be able to walk out of the wilderness with some additional support. If, even with a knee immobilizer, the knee still feels unstable and prone to buckling with weight, the victim should be evacuated without walking (see Appendix C). The victim should see an orthopedic surgeon as soon as possible.

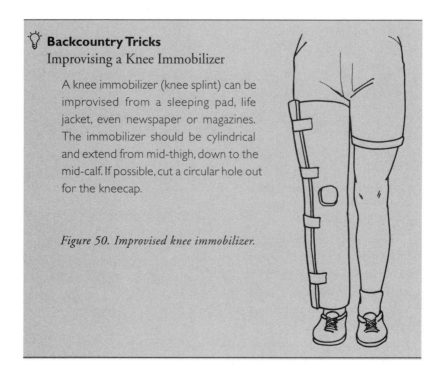

💡 **Backcountry Tricks**
Improvising a Knee Immobilizer

A knee immobilizer (knee splint) can be improvised from a sleeping pad, life jacket, even newspaper or magazines. The immobilizer should be cylindrical and extend from mid-thigh, down to the mid-calf. If possible, cut a circular hole out for the kneecap.

Figure 50. Improvised knee immobilizer.

Torn Menisci (Cartilage)

Menisci are crescent-shaped pieces of cartilage that rest between the femur (thigh bone) and tibia (the larger lower-leg bone) and act as shock absorbers for the knee. Partial and total tears of the menisci often occur at the same time that ligaments around the knee are torn.

SIGNS AND SYMPTOMS

- The single most common symptom of meniscal injury is pain localized to one side of the knee joint that is made worse by walking.
- Catching, clicking, or locking of the knee may be present.
- Occasionally the knee joint can become locked in a partially flexed (bent) and painful position, and the victim will not be able to move the knee or walk.

TREATMENT

1. Treatment is rest, ice (see p. 104) and ibuprofen (Motrin® 600 mg three times a day with food).
2. If the knee feels unstable, wrap a protective immobilizer around the knee (see above).
3. If the victim has a locked knee, attempt to unlock it with traction (see below).

Backcountry Tricks
Unlocking a "Locked Knee"

If the victim has a locked knee, attempt to unlock it by positioning the victim so that his leg hangs over the edge of a table or flat surface with the knee bent in approximately 90 degrees of flexion. After allowing the victim 3 to 5 minutes of relaxation, the rescuer should apply in-line traction by pulling the leg straight down with inward and then outward rotation in an attempt to unlock the joint. Pain medications and muscle relaxers (see Appendix B) may facilitate the manuever.

Patellofemoral Syndrome (Chondromalacia patellae)

This is the most common overuse syndrome of the knee and results in degeneration of the cartilage on the undersurface of the kneecap (patella) from too much rubbing against the thigh bone (femur). It leads to "arthritis" in the knee.

SIGNS AND SYMPTOMS

- Dull aching pain under the kneecap or in the center of the knee. The pain is aggravated by climbing or descending hills, and by sitting for long periods with the knees bent.
- The knee may be swollen.
- Grating "Rice Krispies" sounds can often be heard when the knee is flexed (bent) and straightened.

TREATMENT

1. Rest.
2. Ice (see p. 104).
3. Nonsteroidal anti-inflammatory medication such as ibuprofen (Motrin®) 600 mg three times a day with food.
4. A patella tendon band placed around the leg, below the kneecap, may help prevent pain during walking (see below).
5. Using two trekking or ski poles while hiking will help absorb impact on the knees.

 Backcountry Tricks
Improvising a Patella Tendon Band

To improvise a patella tendon band, roll a bandanna or triangular bandage tightly in on its long axis. Wrap this around the leg just below the kneecap and tie it securely.

Illiotibial Band Syndrome

This is an irritation of the connective tissue along the outside of the thigh.

SIGNS AND SYMPTOMS

- A stinging pain along the outside of the knee that is aggravated by running downhill or jumping.
- Pressing on the outside of the upper knee reproduces the pain.

TREATMENT

1. Rest.
2. Ice (see p. 104).
3. Nonsteroidal anti-inflammatory medication such as ibuprofen (Motrin®) 600 mg every 8 hours with food.

CHAPTER 15

Wounds:
Cuts and Abrasions

A WOUND CAN BE ANYTHING FROM A small skin abrasion to a large cut (laceration). Effective wound management is not difficult to learn, and it comes in handy both in the backcountry and at home. It can often save you a costly and lengthy trip to the emergency room.

Cuts

Cuts are one of the most common reasons that backpackers abort their trips prematurely. Knowing how to clean and close a cut may save your next outing.

SIGNS AND SYMPTOMS
- A break in the skin in which the wound edges can be pulled apart.
- Bleeding.

TREATMENT

There are five sequential steps to follow for treating almost all cuts.

1. Stop the bleeding.
2. Clean the cut.
3. Close the cut.
4. Dress the cut.
5. Check the cut daily for signs of infection.

Step 1: Stop the Bleeding. Almost all bleeding can be controlled by applying pressure directly on the bleeding site. It might be necessary to hold pressure for up to 30 minutes to prevent further bleeding (see p. 24). Elevation of an extremity, in conjunction with direct pressure, may be helpful.

If bleeding from an extremity cannot be stopped by direct pressure, and the victim is in danger of bleeding to death, apply a tourniquet (see p. 25).

Backcountry Tricks
Stopping Bleeding with Nasal Spray or a Tea Bag

Nasal sprays such as Afrin® and NeoSynephrine® contain potent blood vessel constrictors that can help stop bleeding in minor wounds. Simply moisten a 4 by 4 inch piece of sterile gauze with the spray, then pack the gauze into the wound. Leave in place for 5 minutes then remove. The tannic acid in nonherbal tea is also a good blood vessel constrictor and can be used in place of the spray.

Step 2: Clean the Wound. The moment skin is injured, bacteria begin to multiply inside a wound, and any blood and damaged tissue left in the wound create a feeding frenzy for hungry germs. The goal of wound cleansing, therefore, is to prevent infection by ridding the wound of as much bacteria, dirt, and damaged tissue as possible.

The best cleansing method is to use a high-pressure stream of disinfected water (see below) to wash out the bacteria and debris. You can use the disinfected water as is, or you can use it as the base for an improvised saline solution (see below).

A 10- to 15-ml syringe with an 18-gauge catheter tip attached to the end, used like a squirt gun, creates an ideal water pressure of 7 pounds per square inch at the wound surface, which is forceful enough to flush out germs without harming the tissues. (A bulb syringe can only muster a pressure of 0.5 pound per square inch, making it ineffective for wound cleansing.)

To irrigate the wound:

1. Draw the disinfected solution into a 10- to 15-ml syringe (fig. 51A) and attach an 18-gauge catheter tip (fig. 51B).
2. Hold the syringe so the catheter tip is just above the wound and perpendicular to the skin surface.
3. Push down forcefully on the plunger while prying open the edges of the wound with your gloved fingers, and squirt the solution into the wound (fig. 51C). Be careful to avoid getting splashed by the irrigant as it hits the skin (put on a pair of sunglasses or goggles to help protect your eyes from the spray).
4. Repeat this procedure until you have irrigated the wound with at least 400 ml (about 1¾ cups of solution or 30 to 40 syringes full, depending on the size of the syringe). The more you use the better. Remember, "the solution to pollution is dilution."

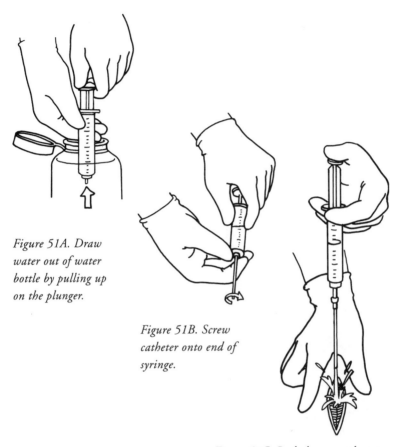

*Figure 51A. Draw
water out of water
bottle by pulling up
on the plunger.*

*Figure 51B. Screw
catheter onto end of
syringe.*

*Figure 51C. Push down on plunger
forcefully to begin irrigation.*

5. Inspect the irrigated wound for any residual particles of dirt or dried blood, and if present, carefully pick them out with tweezers. This is crucial because even one or two particles of dirt left in a wound will increase the likelihood of infection.

6. Control any renewed bleeding by direct pressure on the wound (see step 1).

Note: Once-popular wound-cleansing agents such as hydrogen peroxide and Betadine® (a 10 percent povidone-iodine solution) are useful for cleaning intact skin and removing dried blood and dirt from *around* a wound but should never be poured directly into a break in the skin because they are destructive to delicate tissues and can delay healing. (Betadine®, however, can be used to disinfect water for irrigation.)

∅ Backcountry Tricks
Disinfecting Water to Irrigate a Wound

The liquid you use to irrigate a wound should be clean and nontoxic to the tissues. Although a sterile saline solution is typically used in a hospital setting, in a backcountry situation you can use surface water, disinfecting it as you would for drinking. If you have 10 percent povidone iodine solution (Betadine®), add 50 drops to a half liter (or quart) of water and allow it to sit for at least 15 minutes before using.

Improvising a Saline Solution

To create a saline solution for wound or eye irrigation, add 9 grams of salt (roughly 1 tablespoon) to 1 liter of disinfected water to create a normal (0.9 percent) saline solution.

Using a Plastic Bag to Irrigate a Wound

If you don't have a syringe and catheter, a clean plastic sandwich or garbage bag and a safety pin will do. Fill the bag with irrigation solution and puncture the bottom of the bag with the safety pin. Enlarge the hole by puncturing it a second time. Hold the bag just above the wound and squeeze the top firmly to begin irrigating. Although better than a bulb syringe, this method is less effective than a syringe and catheter because it doesn't generate as much pressure.

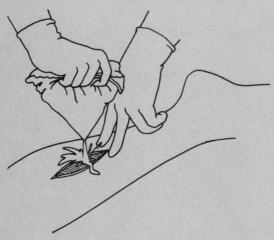

Figure 52. Wound irrigation using a plastic bag.

Step 3: Close the Wound. Many cuts can be closed safely in the backcountry. Time is a critical factor, however, and the longer you delay closure, the more likely the wound is to become infected after it is closed. *The golden period for closing most wounds is within 8 hours after the injury occurs.* If you wait longer, bacteria multiply inside the wound to a dangerous level, and swelling progresses and interferes with the body's defense system. Face and scalp wounds can be safely closed up to 24 hours after the injury, because these areas are more resistant to infection.

Some wounds always carry a high risk of infection, regardless of when they are closed. Examples are wounds inflicted by animal or human bites, puncture wounds, deep wounds on the hands or feet, and those wounds that contain a great deal of crushed or dead tissue.

Most high-risk wounds, and those that have aged beyond the golden period, are best left open and packed with sterile 4 by 4 inch gauze dressings moistened with saline solution or disinfected water. Cover the packed wound with a roller bandage or an Ace® elastic bandage and splint the extremity (see p. 77). A 5-day course of antibiotics such as cephalexin (Keflex® 500 mg every 6 hours) should be taken (see Appendix B). The packing should be changed at least once a day, and medical care should be obtained as soon as possible.

Otherwise, the preferred way to close a cut in the backcountry is with the use of wound closure tape strips or butterfly bandages. Wound closure strips are preferred because they are stronger, longer, stickier, and more porous than butterfly bandages.

To close the wound with wound closure strips:

1. Use scissors to clip off hair near the wound so the tape will adhere better. Hair farther from the wound edge can be shaved. Avoid shaving hair right next to the wound edge as shaving abrades the skin and increases the potential of an infection.
2. Use a cotton swab to apply a thin layer of tincture of benzoin evenly along both sides of the wound, being careful not to get the solution into the wound (it stings) (fig. 53A). The stickiness of the benzoin will help keep the tape in place.
3. After the benzoin dries (about 30 seconds), remove a wound closure strip from its backing (fig. 53B). Place the tape on one side of the wound and use the other end of the tape as a handle to pull the wound closed (fig. 53C). Try not to squeeze the wound edges tightly together—they should just touch. Attach the other end of the tape to the skin to keep the wound closed. The tape should overlap the wound edge by about 1 inch or so on each side.
4. Apply more tape as needed, with a gap of about ¼ inch between each strip (fig. 53D).

5. Place pieces of tape crossways (perpendicular to the other strips) over the ends of the existing strips to keep the ends of the tape from curling up (fig. 53E).
6. Leave the tape in place 7 to 10 days.

Large gaping cuts and wounds that cross a joint are difficult to tape closed and may require suturing. In these instances, get professional medical care as soon as possible. Scalp lacerations can often be closed by tying the victim's hair together (see fig. 15).

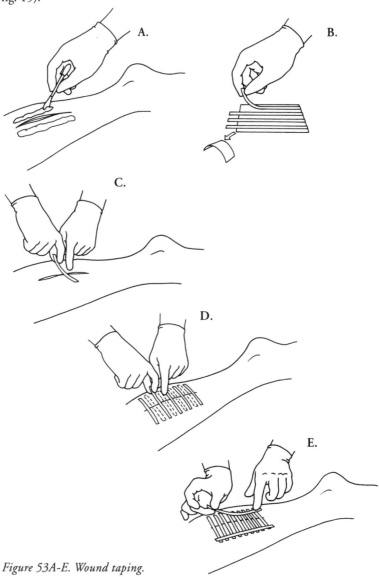

Figure 53A-E. Wound taping.

💡 Backcountry Tricks
Improvising Wound Closure Strips

Wound closure strips can be improvised from duct tape, or other self-adhering tape. Cut ¼-inch strips and then puncture tiny holes along the length of the tape with a safety pin to prevent fluid from building up under the tape.

If you're without tape, you can even glue strips of cloth or nylon from your clothes, pack, or tent to the skin with SuperGlue®. Place a drop of glue on one end of the material and hold it on the skin until it dries. Use the other end to pull the wound closed and glue it onto the skin on the other side of the wound. Avoid getting any glue into the wound. The glue is generally safe on intact skin, but should not be used on the face. Expect the strip to fall off after about 2 to 3 days. If you are still in the backcountry, you can re-apply more strips with fresh glue.

Step 4: Dress the Wound. The best dressing is one that won't stick to the wound. Many nonadherent dressings are available over the counter, including Aquaphor®, Xeroform®, Adaptic®, and Telfa®.

Apply a nonadherent dressing to the wound, and place an absorbent gauze dressing over the nonadherent one. Wrap an elastic bandage or conforming roller bandage around the wound as shown to hold the dressings in place (see fig. 54).

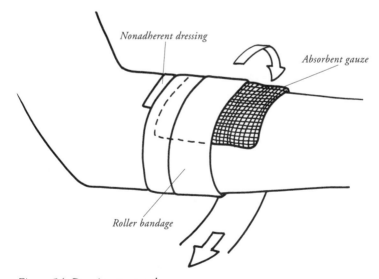

Nonadherent dressing

Absorbent gauze

Roller bandage

Figure 54. Dressing a wound.

☼ Backcountry Tricks
Improvising a Nonadherent Dressing

You can make a nonadherent dressing by spreading Polysporin® or other antibiotic ointment, Vaseline®, or even honey over one side of a sterile 4 by 4 inch gauze dressing.

Honey—"Nature's Neosporin"

Honey can be used on the surface of cuts, abrasions, burns, and frostbite (do not put it directly into a cut) to speed healing and decrease the likelihood of an infection developing.

Improvising a Roller Bandage

You can improvise a conforming roller bandage (one that will conform to the shape of the limb and hold a dressing in place) from a shirt or other article of clothing by cutting a thin strip of material in a circular fashion around the garment. To get the maximum length, cut on the bias (diagonal) of the material.

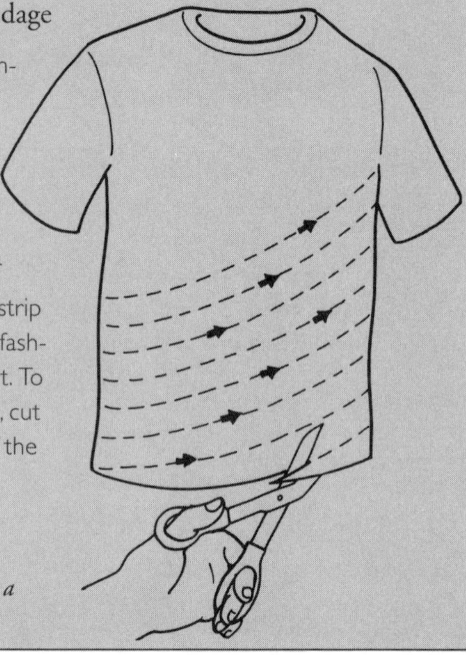

Figure 55. Improvising a roller bandage by cutting a T-shirt in a spiral.

Step 5: Check the Wound Daily for Signs and Symptoms of Infection. Even wounds closed under ideal medical conditions have about a 5 percent chance of becoming infected, so check daily for the following signs and symptoms of infection (fig. 56):

- Increasing pain, redness, or swelling.
- Pus or greenish drainage from the wound.

- Red streaks on the skin adjacent to or above (upstream from) the wound.
- Fever.

If signs or symptoms of infection develop, remove any wound closures (tape or staples) and spread the wound edges open to allow drainage. Place a gauze pad moistened with saline or water inside the wound and cover it with a conforming roller bandage. Change the packing in the wound twice a day. If available, administer antibiotics such as cephalexin (Keflex®) 500 mg every 6 hours for 7 to 10 days. Evacuate the victim to a medical facility as soon as possible.

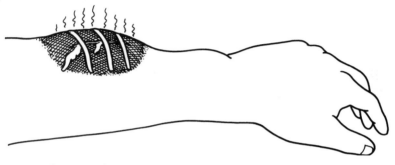

Figure 56. Signs and symptoms of infection.

Abrasions

An abrasion, commonly referred to as a road rash, occurs when the outer layer of skin is scraped off. Abrasions are often embedded with dirt, gravel, and other debris, which if not removed can result in scarring of the skin or infection.

SIGNS AND SYMPTOMS

- Only the outer layer of skin has been scraped away.
- The wound often appears cherry red.
- Bleeding may occur.
- The wound is typically quite painful.
- Dirt and debris may be embedded in the wound.

TREATMENT

To prevent scarring and infection, an abrasion must be vigorously scrubbed with a surgical brush or cleansing pad until all dirt and debris are removed. Be forewarned that this scrubbing can be more painful to the victim than the accident itself.

1. To lessen the pain of the scrubbing, it helps to first spread a topical anesthetic (such as 2 to 4 percent Xylocaine® jelly) over the wound, or wipe the area with a cleansing pad containing lidocaine (another topical anesthetic).

2. Scrub the wound vigorously with a surgical brush or cleansing pad until all foreign materials are removed.
3. Use tweezers to pick out any remaining embedded dirt or debris.
4. Irrigate the abrasion with saline solution (see above) or disinfected water.
5. Apply a thin layer of aloe vera gel or Polysporin® over the abrasion to reduce inflammation and promote healing.
6. Apply a nonadherent protective dressing (see above) and secure it in place with a bandage. You can hold the nonadherent dressing in place with a stockinette bandage (fig. 57) or conforming roller bandage and leave it in place for several days as long as there is no sign of infection.

Figure 57. Stockinette bandage holding a dressing in place over a joint.

CHAPTER 16

Burns

THE MOST COMMON BURN SUSTAINED in the backcountry is the sunburn. Just a few bad sunburns can double your risk of melanoma—the most deadly form of skin cancer. Other common sources of burns in the backcountry include camp stoves and lanterns, cooking in the tent, spilling hot liquids, or campfires. Climbers and rafters are susceptible to rope burns.

PREVENTION

Sunburn can be prevented by wearing protective clothing and using sunscreens or sunblock (see below).

Gasoline, naphtha, propane, and butane fuels used for stoves and lanterns are all highly volatile and can easily turn into an invisible gas that is heavier than air. If the flame in a stove goes out, the gas vapor may continue to discharge out of the stove and collect on the floor of a tent. This collected gas can produce a fiery explosion when a match is lit to reignite the stove, resulting in severe burns. Avoid cooking inside your tent if possible.

Sun Protection

The sun's ultraviolet (UV) rays are most harmful during the summer months, particularly between 10:00 A.M. and 3:00 P.M. Always use sun protection, even on overcast days. (About 80 percent of the sun's rays still reach the earth on a cloudy day, and the effect of UV rays—unlike infrared rays, which produce the sensation of heat—can't be felt.) There are two basic types of sun protection: (1) *sunblocks,* which physically block the sun by reflecting radiation, and (2) *sunscreens,* which use chemicals to absorb and disperse UV rays. Sunblocks tend to be more visible on the skin and are more effective than sunscreens. A sunblock is also less likely to irritate the skin or to cause an allergic reaction. A sunscreen that offers protection against both UVA and UVB rays is preferable.

Sunscreens come with a sun protection factor (SPF) number, which indicates how many times longer the sun will take to burn the skin than if the skin went unprotected. You should use sunscreens with a sun protection factor (SPF) of at least 15 and apply them 15 to 30 minutes before going out into the sun (sunscreens are more effective if they have time to absorb into the skin). Even sunscreens that claim to be waterproof should be reapplied every 1 to 2 hours.

Use a sunscreen with an SPF higher than 15 if you are at a high altitude (above 10,000 feet), or in the snow or water above 5,000 feet. For every 1,000 feet of elevation increase, you are exposed to 4 percent more ultraviolet radiation. Water can reflect up to 90 percent of UV radiation when the sun is directly overhead, essentially doubling the amount that reaches your skin. Snow and sand reflect an additional 80 and 17 percent of UV radiation respectively.

Protective Clothing

Protective clothing is also important in the war against sun damage. Ideally you should wear long-sleeved shirts, long pants, and a wide-brimmed hat. The degree of sun protection offered by clothes is primarily a function of how tightly woven the fabric is. Although a cotton T-shirt will provide good protection (equivalent to an SPF of 12), when it becomes wet it also becomes more translucent and provides significantly less protection. A simple rule of thumb is to hold the fabric up to the light. The more light that comes through, the less protective is the fabric.

National Weather Service UV Index

The National Weather Service is now reporting a UV index to help people plan outdoor activities and avoid exposure to excessive ultraviolet radiation. The index predicts the next day's levels of exposure to UV rays on a scale of 0 to 15.

Index Number	Exposure Level
0–2	Minimal
3–4	Low
5–6	Moderate
7–9	High
10+	Very High

For more information or a UV Index brochure, call the U.S. Environmental Agency, 1-800-296-1996.

BURNS

First-aid treatment and the decision as to whether or not evacuation is necessary depends both on the degree of the burn and the size of the burned area in proportion to the victim's total body surface.

Estimating the Size of a Burn

It is important to determine the extent or size of the burned area, because it helps to guide the treatment plan and predicts the prognosis for recovery. There are two guidelines for estimating the size of the burn: the Rule of Nines which works well for adults, but not for babies or small children; and the Rule of Palms which can be used for small areas in adults or for burns in babies or children.

Rule of Nines

The Rule of Nines divides the adult body into areas, each of which represents 9 percent (or a multiple thereof) of the total body surface area (TBSA). To estimate the percentage of the body that is covered by a burn, refer to figure 58 and add up the percentages or partial percentages of the areas affected.

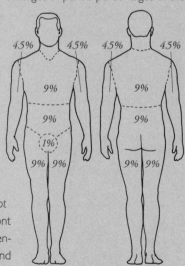

- Each arm = 9 percent
- Each leg = 18 percent
- Chest = 9 percent
- Abdomen = 9 percent
- Upper back = 9 percent
- Lower back = 9 percent
- Head and neck = 9 percent
- Perineum (genital area) = 1 percent

For example, a victim with a burn involving the entire face, but *not* the back of the head (4½%), the front and back of the left arm (9%), the entire chest and upper back (18%), and half of the back of one leg (4½%) would have a TBSA burn of 36%.

Figure 58. Body divisions according to the Rule of Nines.

Rule of Palms

A person's palm covers an area roughly equivalent to 1 percent of his body surface area. You can use the size of the victim's palm as a measure to estimate the percentage of body area burned.

GENERAL TREATMENT GUIDELINES

1. Apply cool water to the area. Do not overcool the victim and produce hypothermia. Ice should not be used except on very small burns.
2. Remove all burned clothing from the victim.
3. Assess the airway to make sure it is not blocked, and complete a primary survey (see pp. 15–16).
4. Remove any jewelry from burned hands or feet.
5. For chemical burns, flush the site with large amounts of disinfected water for at least 15 minutes.
6. A victim with a burn greater than 20 percent TBSA (see above) can lose a great deal of fluids from burned tissues and go into shock (see p. 33). If he is not vomiting and has a normal level of consciousness, try to encourage him to drink fluids.
7. A burn injury encompassing less than 5 percent of the victim's total body surface area (excluding a second-degree burn of the face, hands, feet, genitals, or one that completely encircles an extremity) can be treated in a wilderness setting if adequate first-aid supplies are available and if wound care is performed diligently.

Burns are classified into first-, second-, and third-degree burns according to the depth of the burn as follows:

First-Degree Burns

First-degree, or superficial, burns involve only the outermost layer of the skin. Sunburn and coffee spills are typically first-degree burns.

SIGNS AND SYMPTOMS

- The skin is red.
- Pain may range from mild to severe.
- No blisters are present.

TREATMENT

1. See General Treatment Guidelines (above).
2. Apply aloe vera gel to the burn.
3. Nonsteroidal anti-inflammatory drugs such as ibuprofen (Motrin®), 800 mg three times a day with food for 3 days, will help relieve pain and speed healing.
4. First-degree burns rarely require evacuation.

Second-Degree Burns

Second-degree burns are deeper than first-degree burns and involve both the superficial and middle layers of the skin.

SIGNS AND SYMPTOMS
- The skin is red.
- Blisters are present, but may not occur for several hours following injury.
- The burned area is quite painful and sensitive to touch.

TREATMENT
1. See General Treatment Guidelines (above).
2. Irrigate the burn gently with cool, disinfected water or saline solution (see p. 116) to remove all loose dirt and skin.
3. Peel off or trim away any loose skin with a scissors.
4. Puncture the blister with a sterile safety pin (see below) and drain the fluid from any blister larger than 2.5 cm (1 inch). Then trim the dead skin away with a scissors. Leave small, thick blisters intact.
5. Apply aloe vera gel, or an antibiotic ointment to the burn.
6. Cover the burn with a nonadherent dressing (see p. 119), such as Spenco 2nd Skin ®, Telfa®, or Xeroform®. Change the dressing at least once a day.
7. A nonsteroidal anti-inflammatory drug such as ibuprofen (Motrin®), 800 mg three times a day with food for 3 days, will help relieve pain and speed healing.

To Sterilize Needles or Other Implements Do One of the Following:
- Hold in a flame until red-hot.
- Place in boiling water for 2 minutes.
- Place in 10 percent povidone iodine for 5 minutes.

 Backcountry Tricks
Improvising a Burn Dressing
Medical research has shown that a gauze pad impregnated with honey is an effective covering for burn wounds. It reduces the incidence of infection and promotes healing of the wound.

Third-Degree Burns
Third-degree burns are the most serious burns. They involve all layers of the skin, including nerves, blood vessels, and even muscle. Third-degree burns require skin grafting.

SIGNS AND SYMPTOMS

- Pain is absent because the nerve endings have been destroyed. Second-degree burns adjacent to a third-degree burn, however, will still produce pain.
- The skin is usually dry, leathery, firm, and charred, and is insensitive to light touch or a pinprick.

TREATMENT

1. See General Treatment Guidelines (above).
2. Follow treatment guidelines for second-degree burns.
3. Watch for shock and treat if it occurs (see p. 33).
4. Evacuate the victim as soon as possible to a medical facility (see Appendix C).

💣 WHEN TO WORRY
Severe Burns

Severe burns can lead to shock. With any of the following burns, evacuate the victim to a medical center immediately (see Appendix C).

- Second-degree burns greater than 20 percent of total body area (TBSA)
- Third-degree burns greater than 10 percent TBSA
- Burns involving the hands, face, feet, or genitals
- Burns complicated by smoke inhalation
- Electrical burns
- Burns in infants and the elderly

People with facial burns, singed nasal hairs, carbonaceous (black) sputum, hoarseness, or wheezing should also be evacuated immediately. They are in danger of developing an obstructed airway from severe swelling in their throat and windpipe.

CHAPTER 17

Venomous Snake
and Lizard Bites

VENOMOUS SNAKE AND LIZARD BITES can produce a wide range of manifestations, from mild, local reactions to severe, life-threatening toxicity.

Approximately 8,000 venomous snakebites occur in the United States each year, with 10 to 20 deaths. Forty percent of snakebites are not accidental; they occur when a poisonous snake is purposely handled. Your chance of dying from a venomous snakebite in the wilderness is minuscule (about 1 in 12 million).

All forty-eight contiguous states except Maine have at least one species of venomous snake. There are no venomous snakes in Hawaii or Alaska. The states with the highest incidence of snakebite are North Carolina, Arkansas, Texas, Mississippi, Louisiana, Arizona, and New Mexico. About 90 percent of snakebites occur between April and October, since snakes are more active in warm months.

The only two species of venomous lizard in the world are found in North America. The Gila monster *(Heloderma suspectum)* and the Mexican beaded lizard *(Heloderma horridum)* both possess venom glands and grooved teeth capable of envenomating humans.

PREVENTION

Do not try to pick up or capture snakes or lizards. Walk on clearly marked trails, and use a walking stick to move suspicious objects. Do not reach into areas that you cannot see first. Keep your tent zipped up tight at night. Gather firewood while it is still light or use a flashlight and caution at night.

Wear high, thick boots while traveling in snake country. Snakes can strike up to half their body length—keep your distance. If you hear the sound of a rattlesnake, freeze, locate the snake, and back away slowly.

VENOMOUS SNAKES

There are two classes of poisonous snakes indigenous to the United States:

- *Pit vipers (crotalidae)*—rattlesnakes, cottonmouths (water moccasins), and copperheads—have a characteristic triangular head, a deep pit (heat receptor organ) between the eye and nostril, and a catlike, elliptical pupil.
- *Coral snakes (elapidae)* are characterized by red, black, and yellow or white bands encircling the body. The fangs are very short. These snakes bite by chewing rather than by striking.

☀ Pit Vipers

Pit vipers generally strike only once and usually from a coiled position. The snake's striking range is roughly a distance corresponding to one half of the length of its body. Approximately 20 to 30 percent of bites are so-called "dry bites," in which no venom is injected.

SIGNS AND SYMPTOMS OF ENVENOMATION

One or more of the following signs and symptoms may occur.

- One or more fang marks (rattlesnake bites may leave one, two, or even three fang marks) should be visible.
- Burning at the site of the bite immediately after the strike.
- Swelling at the site of the bite occurs within 5 to 20 minutes and spreads slowly over a period of 6 to 12 hours. The faster the swelling progresses up the arm or leg, the worse the degree of envenomation.
- Bruising (black-and-blue discoloration) and blister formation at the bite site.
- Numbness and tingling of the lips and face, usually 10 to 60 minutes after the bite.
- Twitching of the eye muscles and muscles around the mouth.
- Some victims complain of a rubbery or metallic taste in the mouth.
- After 6 to 12 hours, bleeding from the gums and nose may develop, denoting a serious envenomation.
- Weakness, sweating, nausea, vomiting, and faintness.
- Most deaths occur 6 to 48 hours after the bite. Only about 5 percent of deaths occur within the first hour of envenomation and are probably related to the direct injection of venom into a blood vessel.

TREATMENT

The definitive treatment for snake venom poisoning is the administration of antivenin. The most important thing you can do is to get the victim to a medical facility as quickly as possible. "If you do nothing in the field for a snakebite victim—you've done nothing wrong."

1. Back out of the snake's striking range, which is at least one-half the length of the snake.

2. It is not necessary to kill the snake and transport it with the victim for identification, but if you do kill the snake, do not pick it up with your bare hands, and be sure to transport it in a closed container. Decapitated snake heads can still envenomate an individual.

3. Rinse the area around the bite site with water to remove any venom that might remain on the surface of the skin.

4. Clean the wound (see p. 114) and cover with a sterile dressing (see p. 119).

5. Remove all of the victim's rings and jewelry, as severe swelling may soon occur.

6. If possible, splint the injured part in a functional position as you would for a fracture (see p. 77), and position it just below the level of the heart.

7. Transport the victim to the nearest hospital as soon as possible (see Appendix C). If you pass a telephone, stop and notify the hospital that you are bringing in a snakebite victim so they can begin to locate and procure antivenin.

OTHER FIRST-AID TREATMENTS THAT MAY BE BENEFICIAL

The Sawyer Extractor®. The Sawyer Extractor® (fig. 59) may remove up to 30 percent of the venom if used within 3 minutes after a snakebite. The device comes with four different-size suction cups that attach to the barrel of the supplied syringe. Because of the high negative pressure obtained with this device, an incision over the bite site is *not* required.

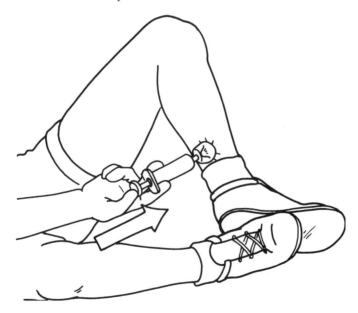

Figure 59. Using the Sawyer Extractor®.

1. Choose a suction cup size that will cover the entire bite site and attach it to the syringe.
2. Pull the plunger of the syringe out to its full length.
3. Place the cup and syringe unit over the bite site and push the plunger all the way down, thus creating negative pressure over the bite site. If the unit has been applied properly, you will see blood-tinged yellow fluid emerging from the fang marks into the cup.
4. When the cup fills with fluid, remove the extractor, rinse the fluid away, and reapply the device in the same manner as before.
5. Suction should be applied within 3 minutes of the bite and should be continued for 30 minutes for maximum effectiveness.

Australian Compression and Immobilization Technique. In the Australian compression and immobilization technique, the entire bitten extremity is immediately wrapped with a broad elastic bandage and then splinted with any available object. This method has proven effective in the treatment of coral and sea snake envenomations and may also help delay absorption of pit viper venom. Unfortunately, with pit viper envenomation, this treatment may also worsen local tissue damage at the bite site. It is only recommended in pit viper envenomations when the victim appears to have suffered a severe envenomation and is several hours from medical care.

1. Begin applying a circumferential elastic bandage (such as an Ace® bandage) at the bite site, wrapping it upward toward the torso in an even fashion, about as tightly as you would wrap a sprained ankle (fig. 60).
2. Monitor the color, pulse, and temperature of the hand or foot to make sure that there is adequate circulation. If circulation appears compromised (the skin turns white or blue and becomes cold, the pulse becomes diminished, and the victim feels numbness or tingling), loosen the wrap. Otherwise the bandage should not be released until the victim is under the care of a physician at a medical facility.
3. Immobilize the limb with a well-padded splint.

WHAT *NOT* TO DO
The following treatments have no proven benefit and may worsen the situation and cause further harm to the victim.

• Do not make any incisions in the skin or apply suction with your mouth.
• Do not apply ice or a tourniquet. Ice can cause further tissue damage and does not delay the absorption of, or inactivate, snake venom.
• Do not shock the victim with a stun gun or electrical current. There is no scientific evidence that electrical shock is of any value for the treatment of snakebites.

- The use of antivenin in the field is discouraged. Carrying the extensive equipment and drugs necessary to provide intravenous antivenin is cumbersome, and severe anaphylactic shock can occur following the administration of antivenin.

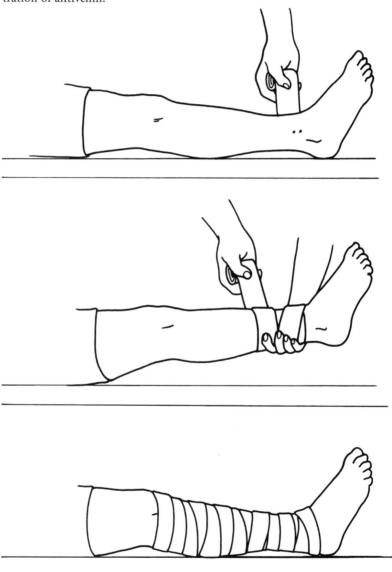

Figure 60. The Australian compression and immobilization technique.

☀ Coral Snakes

Coral snakes include two species, the Arizona coral snake *(Micruroides euryxanthus),* found mostly in New Mexico and Arizona, and the Eastern coral snake *(Micrurus fulvius),* located primarily in North Carolina and the Gulf Coast states. Approximately 60 percent of coral snakebites do not lead to any envenomation.

SIGNS AND SYMPTOMS OF ENVENOMATION

- Initially there is a slight burning pain at the site of the bite.
- Within 90 minutes, numbness and/or weakness of the bitten arm or leg develops.
- In 1 to 3 hours, the victim develops twitching, nervousness, drowsiness, increased salivation, and drooling.
- Within 5 to 10 hours, the victim develops slurred speech, double vision, difficulty talking and swallowing, and difficulty breathing. The venom may cause total paralysis or death. Symptoms may sometimes be delayed by up to 13 hours after the bite.

TREATMENT

First-aid treatment is the same as for a pit viper bite. Early use of the compression and immobilization technique (see above) is highly recommended because it is both effective and safe (coral snake venom does not produce any local tissue destruction).

Venomous Lizards

The Gila monster *(Heloderma suspectum)* and Mexican beaded lizard *(Heloderma horridum)* are found only in the Great Sonoran Desert area in southern Arizona and northwestern Mexico. Not all bites result in envenomation, since the lizard may only nip the victim or not expel any venom during a bite.

Gila monsters may hang on tenaciously during a bite, and pliers, or a sharp knife, may be required to loosen the grip of its jaws.

SIGNS AND SYMPTOMS OF ENVENOMATION

- Pain and severe burning is felt at the wound site within 5 minutes and may radiate (spread) up the extremity. Intense pain may last from 3 to 5 hours and then subside after 8 hours.
- Swelling occurs at the wound site, usually within 15 minutes, and progresses slowly up the extremity. Blue discoloration may appear around the wound.
- The victim may feel weak and faint and may start sweating.
- The wound site may remain tender for 3 to 4 weeks after the bite, but there is rarely any permanent tissue damage.

TREATMENT

1. Clean the wound thoroughly as you would for any laceration (see p. 114).
2. Inspect the wound and remove any shed or broken teeth.
3. The extremity should be splinted in a functional position and elevated to help decrease pain and swelling.
4. The victim should be given a tetanus shot if he has not had one in the last 5 years.

CHAPTER 18

Insect and Spider Bites and Stings

BITING AND STINGING INSECTS AND spiders are found worldwide. They can cause local reactions and infections at the bite site, severe allergic reactions such as anaphylactic shock, or poisoning from their venom. Many infectious diseases such as malaria, dengue fever, and Lyme disease (see below) are contracted through the bite of an insect.

PREVENTION

Protection against insect and spider bites is important in the wilderness and especially important in the tropics. In insect-laden areas, wear protective clothing, especially from dusk to dawn, when many insects are more apt to feed. When practical, wear garments made of thick, tightly woven fabrics with high necklines, long sleeves, and long trousers. Wear a bandanna around your neck and cover your head with a hat. Many insects can bite through flimsy cloth, especially when you bend or stretch. The best colors for garments are light green, white, tan, and khaki. Insects seem to be more attracted to dark colors. Wear high socks and shoes or sneakers, not sandals. At dusk, tuck your pants into your socks or shoes, and tape the cuffs of your shirt sleeves closed. Consider ankle and wrist bands impregnated with permethrin (see below). Spraying footwear and clothing with permethrin is also helpful. Check yourself and your companions for ticks at least every 4 hours when walking in tick-infested areas.

Make yourself unattractive to insects. Looking and smelling like a flower attracts insects. Avoid perfumes and hair sprays.

Choose campsites that are high and dry and away from rotting wood. Screens, mosquito nets, and insect repellents should be used at night. Dipping or spraying the nets with permethrin prior to use greatly increases their effectiveness. Cover food, utensils, and garbage. Shake out clothing and shoes before putting them on.

Insect Repellents

What Works. The most effective repellents contain concentrations of 20 to 30 percent DEET (N-N, diethyl-toluamide). The duration of action is between 2 and 6 hours, depending on the concentration of DEET, how much the wearer perspires, and how hungry the insect is. Apply only a thin layer; thicker coats are not more protective and may increase chances of toxicity. There have been rare reports of adverse reactions to DEET, ranging from skin rashes to central nervous system (brain) disorders.

When using DEET in conjunction with sunscreens, apply the sunscreen first, about 30 minutes prior to sun exposure. Apply the DEET over the sunscreen. Cover all exposed skin with a thin, uniform layer of repellent. Do not rub it into the skin.

Do not use DEET on infants less than 1 year of age, and minimize the amount used on children. Preparations with lower concentrations of DEET (7 to 10 percent) in formulations that minimize absorption are available. DEET has not been studied in pregnant women. Studies in animals show that it crosses the placenta and passes into the fetus. It should be avoided or used very sparingly by pregnant or nursing women.

DEET may damage clothing and tents made of leather, rayon, spandex, and other materials.

Permethrin is an insecticide that is generally safe. It is very effective when used on clothing, tents, and mosquito netting. Clothing and tents should be sprayed thoroughly with permethrin prior to your trip and allowed to dry. The protective effect can last up to several weeks and withstand several washings. Permethrin is safe on all garments.

What Doesn't Work. Don't rely on smoke, citronella, Skin-So-Soft®, vitamin B1, and sound-making devices. Citronella and Skin-So-Soft® are weak repellents, and their effect lasts only for about 60 to 90 minutes. Although they may be effective in your backyard for no-see-ums and not-too-hungry mosquitoes, I would not depend on them in the jungle or in the backcountry, where infection-carrying insects thrive.

GENERAL SIGNS AND SYMPTOMS OF BITES AND STINGS

- Insect bites and stings are generally painful and produce local inflammation (redness, swelling) at the site.
- Occasionally, venom from insects and spiders can produce severe allergic reactions and lead to life-threatening anaphylactic shock (see p. 36).

GENERAL TREATMENT GUIDELINES FOR BITES AND STINGS

1. Apply ice or cold packs to the bite site to help alleviate local pain and swelling.
2. Swabbing the bite with an Insect Sting Relief Swab® (active ingredient is 6 percent benzocaine) may help relieve pain.

3. Oral antihistamines, such as diphenhydramine (Benadryl®), 25 to 50 mg every 4 hours, are helpful in relieving the itching, rash, and swelling associated with many insect and spider bites and stings.

4. The principles of wound care (see p. 113) apply to bites and stings as well. Any bite or sting can become infected and should therefore be examined at regular intervals for progressive redness, swelling, pain, or drainage of pus.

Bee and Wasp Stings

Honeybees leave a stinger and venom sack in the victim after a sting. The fact that the bees rip off their hind ends in the process and die is small consolation for the pain they inflict. Hornets, yellow jackets, bumblebees, and wasps do not leave a stinger and may puncture a victim repeatedly.

SIGNS AND SYMPTOMS
- Pain is immediate and may be accompanied by swelling, redness, and warmth at the site.
- In allergic individuals, anaphylactic shock can occur.

TREATMENT
1. Anaphylactic shock must be treated immediately with epinephrine and antihistamines (see p. 36).
2. For honeybee stings, remove the stinger and venom sack as quickly as possible. Even with the rest of the bee gone, the venom sac can still continue to pump more venom into the skin. Do not hesitate or search for a pocketknife or credit card to scrape or tease the stinger out of the skin. Grab that stinger and yank. It is better to remove the stinger quickly than worry about pinching or squeezing more venom from the sac.
3. Apply ice or cold water to the sting site.
4. Anesthetic sprays, swabs, and creams (such as Insect Sting Relief Swab®) may help relieve pain.
5. For adults, diphenhydramine (Benadryl®), 25 to 50 mg every 4 to 6 hours, will help relieve itching, swelling, and redness.

💡 Backcountry Tricks
Relieving Bee and Wasp Stings

For bee venom (which is acid), apply a paste of baking soda and water. For wasp venom (which is alkaline), apply vinegar, lemon juice, or other acidic substance. Meat tenderizer applied locally to the sting site may also be effective in denaturing the venom and relieving pain and inflammation.

SPIDER BITES

Although only some spiders are considered poisonous, all spiders have venom that can produce local pain and inflammation. Generally, spiders will bite you only once. If you see more than one wound, the bite was probably inflicted by an insect and not a spider.

🕷 BlackWidow Spider *(Lactrodectus mactans)*

Black widow spiders are about ⅝ inch long and are black with a red hourglass mark on the underside of the abdomen. They are nocturnal and generally live in wood piles, stone walls, and outhouses.

SIGNS AND SYMPTOMS OF ENVENOMATION

- The initial bite feels like a sharp pinprick but sometimes may even go unnoticed.
- Within 1 hour, the victim may develop a tingling and numbing sensation in the palms of the hands and the bottoms of the feet, along with muscle cramps, particularly in the abdomen (stomach) and back. In severe cases, the stomach muscles may become rigid and boardlike.
- Sweating and vomiting are common, and the victim may complain of headache and weakness.
- The victim's blood pressure can become markedly elevated, and he can develop seizures.

TREATMENT

Untreated, most people recover in 8 to 12 hours. Small children and elderly victims, however, may have severe reactions, occasionally leading to death.

1. See General Treatment Guidelines (above).
2. Apply ice packs to the bite to relieve pain.
3. Prescription muscle relaxers like diazepam (Valium®) 5-10 mg or cyclobenzaprine (Flexeril®) 10 mg will help relieve muscle spasms. Prescription pain relievers like hydrocodone and acetaminophen (Vicodin®) one to two tablets are also helpful.
4. A specific antidote is available at medical facilities for those suffering severe symptoms.

🕷 Brown Recluse Spider *(Loxasceles reclusa)*

The brown recluse spider is found most commonly in the South and the southern part of the Midwest. The spider is brownish, with a body length of just under ½ inch. A characteristic dark, violin-shaped marking is found on the top of the upper section of the body. The brown recluse spider can inject a venom which causes severe local skin destruction at the bite site.

SIGNS AND SYMPTOMS OF ENVENOMATION
- The bite sensation is initially mild, producing the same degree of pain as that of an ant sting. The stinging subsides over 6 to 8 hours and is replaced by aching and itching at the bite site.
- Within 1 to 5 hours, a painful red blister appears, surrounded by a bull's-eye of whitish-blue discoloration.
- Over the next 10 to 14 days, the blister ruptures and a gradually enlarging ulcer crater develops with further destruction of tissue.
- Fever, chills, weakness, nausea, and vomiting may develop within 24 to 48 hours of the bite.

TREATMENT
1. See General Treatment Guidelines (above).
2. Apply ice or cold compresses to the wound initially for pain relief.
3. If the blister has ruptured, apply an antibiotic ointment to the wound and cover with a nonadherent sterile dressing and bandage (see p. 119).
4. The victim should be evacuated to a medical facility as soon as possible (see Appendix C). An antivenin is now available, which when used early can prevent the loss of tissue and scarring.

• • •

Tarantulas

There are approximately 40 species of tarantula in the United States; most are found in the Southwest and in the southeastern States. They are large, slow spiders capable of inflicting a painful bite. The bites sometimes become infected.

SIGNS AND SYMPTOMS OF ENVENOMATION
- Tarantula bites tend to be very painful at the bite site and can produce local swelling and numbness.
- Several Latin American species may flick hairs through the air into a victim's skin and eyes, causing intense burning and itching that may last for days.

TREATMENT
1. See General Treatment Guidelines (above).
2. Apply ice for pain relief.
3. Elevate and immobilize the bitten extremity to reduce pain.
4. Apply an antibiotic ointment (see Appendix B) to the site.
5. Ibuprofen (Motrin®) 600 mg every 8 hours with food or acetaminophen (Tylenol®) 1000 mg every 4 to 6 hours will help relieve pain. Antihistamines such as diphenhydramine (Benadryl®) 25 to 50 mg every 4 to 6 hours will reduce itching.

SCORPION STINGS

Scorpions are nocturnal creatures that hide during the day under bark, in rocky crevices, or burrowed down into the sand. The venom is injected by the stinger in the scorpion's tail. Most North American species are nonlethal, and their stings produce only localized pain and swelling; severe allergic reactions are rare. The pain of a nonlethal species sting is similar to that of a wasp or hornet, and the treatment is similar (see above).

🔥 Bark Scorpion (Centruoides sculpturatus)

The only potentially lethal scorpion found in the United States is the bark scorpion, named for its habit of hiding beneath loose and fallen pieces of tree bark. It is found in the desert areas of the Southwest (Arizona, New Mexico, California, Texas) and northern Mexico. It is usually small (¾ to ½ inch in length), straw-yellow colored, with long slender pincers. The venom contains neurotoxins that can be lethal, but usually only in infants or small children.

SIGNS AND SYMPTOMS OF ENVENOMATION

- Immediate pain, which is worsened by tapping lightly over the bite site.
- Restlessness and involuntary twitching of the muscles, which can progress to shaking and jerking of arms and legs and mimic a seizure.
- Blurred vision and roving eye movements.
- Trouble swallowing, drooling, slurred speech.
- Numbness and tingling around the mouth, feet, and hands.
- Difficulty breathing.

TREATMENT

There is no good first-aid treatment in the wilderness. The goal is to make the victim comfortable:

1. See General Treatment Guidelines (above).
2. Place a piece of ice over the sting area to reduce pain.
3. Evacuate the victim to a medical facility as soon as possible (see Appendix C), as antivenin is available in the areas where lethal scorpions live.

• • •

Fire Ant (Solenopsis invicta)

Fire ants are found in the southeastern states, Texas, and parts of California. They have large heads and long legs, and range in color from a drab yellow to red or black. The ant is tenacious and will sting its victim repeatedly, in as many places as the stinger can reach. The first fire ant to sting will send a signal to others, and the victim may soon find many ants swarming up his leg.

SIGNS AND SYMPTOMS OF ENVENOMATION
- Initially there develops a cluster of small, painful, and itchy blisters. These usually evolve into small pustules (boils) within 24 hours. The skin over the pustule will slough away in 2 to 3 days, after which the sores heal.
- Some victims develop a severe reaction characterized by large, red, swollen welts that are very itchy.
- About 1 percent of fire ant stings are followed by anaphylactic reactions which must be treated immediately (see p. 36).

TREATMENT
1. See General Treatment Guidelines (above).
2. Apply ice or cold packs to the affected area.
3. Administer ibuprofen (Motrin®) 600 mg every 8 hours with food, acetaminophen (Tylenol®) 1000 mg every 4 to 6 hours, or hydrocodone and acetaminophen (Vicodin®) 2 tablets every 4 to 6 hours for pain.
4. The rash and itching can be treated with antihistamines, such as diphenhydramine (Benadryl®) 25 to 50 mg every 4 to 6 hours. Topical steroid creams such as hydrocortisone or triamcinalone may also help to reduce the itching. In severe cases, a physician can prescribe prednisone, a potent anti-inflammatory medicine that will dramatically reduce the itching and rash.

Puss Caterpillar (*Megalopyge opercularis*)

The puss caterpillar, or woolly slug, is found in the southern United States and has venomous bristles that inflict a very painful sting. Envenomation is usually caused by touching the caterpillar while it clings to vegetation.

SIGNS AND SYMPTOMS OF ENVENOMATION
- Contact causes instant pain, followed by redness and swelling at the site.
- Symptoms usually subside within 24 hours.
- In rare cases, nausea, headache, fever, vomiting, and shock (see p. 36) may occur.

TREATMENT
1. See General Treatment Guidelines (above).
2. Pat the skin with a piece of adhesive tape to remove any remaining bristles.
3. The local reaction can be lessened by applying hydrocortisone cream or calamine lotion to the site, and by taking an oral antihistamine such as diphenhydramine (Benadryl®) 25 to 50 mg every 4 to 6 hours.

Centipedes and Millipedes

Centipedes are elongate, flattened arthropods with one pair of legs for each of the body segments, which may number from 15 to more than 100. Most centipedes

live in crevices or beneath objects on the ground. Millipedes differ from centipedes in having two pairs of legs per body segment and generally roll into a ball
when disturbed. Both are found throughout the southern United States.

SIGNS AND SYMPTOMS OF ENVENOMATION

- Centipede bites can produce local swelling, redness, and a burning pain.
  Swelling and pain may persist for as long as 3 weeks or may disappear and
  recur.
- Millipedes do not bite but can secrete a toxic chemical that, when touched,
  produces skin irritation.

TREATMENT

1. Treatment is the same as for fire ants (see above).
2. For millipede reactions, irrigate the site with lots of water.

TICKS

Because of their disease-carrying capabilities, ticks have commanded a great deal
of attention in the press during the past few years. Despite what some people
claim, ticks do not hop or fly onto people and do not hide among tree branches
waiting to drop down in large numbers on an unsuspecting victim. They do,
however, lie in wait on vegetation and are brushed onto people who pass close by.

Ticks are attracted by heat, carbon dioxide, and butyric acid, which is found in
butter, sweat, feces, and urine. Once a tick grabs onto a person, it clings to hair or
clothing and waits for several hours until the individual is at rest. Then it moves to
an exposed area—often around the tops of the socks or at the neckline—attaches
itself, and begins feeding. An anesthetic agent in the tick's saliva usually makes the
"bite" painless. Ticks feed from 2 hours to several days before dropping off.

Ticks don't really bite or sting. They don't even have teeth or stingers. Instead
they have a barb-shaped lower jaw, called a hypostome, which looks something
like a stonemason's trowel. The tick embeds its hypostome into the victim's skin
and eventually reaches a tiny blood vessel. Once embedded, the tick begins to feed
through an opening just behind the mouthparts. In order to thin the blood and
keep it from clotting, the tick secretes a chemical in its saliva into the wound that
prevents the blood from clotting, and in so doing may transmit disease-producing
organisms.

Of the 840 known tick species, about 100 species transmit infections to
man. The most infamous species are the tiny deer tick *(Ixodes scapularis)* and the
black-legged tick *(Ixodes pacificus),* which spread Lyme disease and ehrlichiosis
(see below); the wood tick *(Dermacentor andersoni),* which transmits Rocky
Mountain spotted fever (see below); and the dog tick *(Dermacentor variabilis),*
which transmits ehrlichiosis and Rocky Mountain spotted fever.

Backcountry Tricks
Removing an Embedded Tick

The wrong way: A lot of fiction and friction has been generated over the best way to remove an embedded tick from one's skin. Traditional folk methods for removing ticks—such as applying fingernail polish, petroleum jelly, rubbing alcohol, or a hot match head—increase the chance that the tick will salivate or regurgitate into the wound, thus spreading infection.

The right way:

1. Use a pair of tweezers to grasp the tick as close to the victim's skin as possible, taking care not to crush, squeeze, or puncture the body. Steady, straight upward traction is the best technique for removing the tick. It may take a couple of minutes to convince the tick to let go. Avoid twisting, as it can break off and leave behind mouthparts. The Sawyer Tick Plier® has long, thin jaws that slide easily beneath a tick's body without squeezing it, and stops between the handles that prevent you from cutting the tick.

2. After removal, disinfect the bite site with an antiseptic towelette.

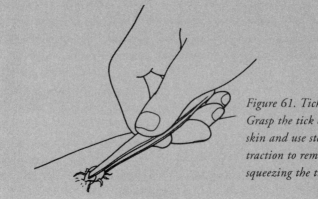

Figure 61. Tick removal. Grasp the tick close to the skin and use steady, upward traction to remove. Avoid squeezing the tick body.

Noninfectious Problems

Tick bites can cause problems without transmitting infectious agents. The bite can be painful, and produce a red puncture wound. Some ticks (the wood tick in the western United States and the dog tick in the eastern United States) secrete a neurotoxin in their saliva which can lead to paralysis. A victim may develop a local allergic reaction at the bite site, and during tick removal parts of the tick may break off and remain embedded in the skin.

SIGNS AND SYMPTOMS

- A painful red and swollen wound may appear at the puncture site, which can take 1 to 2 weeks to heal.
- If a neurotoxin is secreted, the victim can become paralyzed (Tick Paralysis), beginning in the legs and spreading to the arms, trunk, and head. This usually develops only after the tick has been attached for more than 5 days.
- If parts of the tick are left embedded in the skin, a painful nodule may develop.

TREATMENT

1. Treat local reactions such as pain and swelling by applying ice to the site and by taking antihistamines such as diphenhydramine (Benadryl®), 25 to 50 mg every 4 to 6 hours.
2. If Tick Paralysis develops, removal of the tick will abate the symptoms and the victim should recover completely within several hours.
3. Embedded tick parts should be surgically excised by a physician.

Localized Infections

Tick bites can occasionally become infected at the bite site, similar to any other wound.

SIGNS AND SYMPTOMS

- Increasing redness, swelling, and pain at the bite site.
- Drainage of pus.

TREATMENT

Apply a topical antibiotic cream to the wound and administer an oral antibiotic, if available, such as cephalexin (Keflex®), 500 mg every 6 hours (see Appendix B). Seek medical attention as soon as possible.

SYSTEMIC INFECTIONS
Lyme Disease

Lyme disease is an infection caused by a spirochete, a type of bacteria that invades the body during the bite of an infected tick. Called "The Great Imitator" because of its ability to mimic a wide variety of other illnesses, Lyme disease is now the most common tick-transmitted infection, with an estimated 5,000 to 15,000 new cases in the United States each year. Fewer than half of all people with Lyme disease can remember ever having been bitten by a tick.

Lyme disease is transmitted by the deer tick *(Ixodes scapularis)* and the black-legged tick *(Ixodes pacificus)* and has been documented on every continent except Antarctica. It is found all across the United States but is most common in the northeastern coastal states (New York, Connecticut, Pennsylvania, New Jersey, and Rhode Island, in decreasing order, account for most of the reported cases); in the upper Midwest (including Michigan, Wisconsin, and Minnesota); and on the Pacific Coast (California and Oregon).

The adult deer tick is about the size of the lowercase letter *o*. In its immature nymphal stage, it is no larger than a period on this page and resembles a speck of dirt or a freckle. The risk of infection increases the longer the tick is attached to your skin. In areas of the Northeast, 90 percent of the deer ticks are infected with Lyme disease spirochetes. In most West Coast areas tested so far, about 1 to 2 percent of black-legged ticks are infected with the spirochetes.

SIGNS AND SYMPTOMS

Signs and symptoms of Lyme disease can vary greatly from person to person, and there is no absolute predictable time frame or sequence of events. Three general stages are usually designated, corresponding to the time frame and severity of the illness.

Stage one. About 70 percent of infected individuals develop an expanding, circular red rash (erythema migrains) from 3 days to 1 month after the tick bite (7 days is average). As the rash expands, it partially clears in the center while the outer borders remain bright red, giving the appearance of a bull's-eye. The rash may reach a diameter of 15 cm (6 inches) with a range of 3 to 68 cm and may appear in places unrelated to the bite site; the thigh, groin, and armpit are the most common locations. The rash is warm to the touch and usually produces itching or burning. It fades after an average of 28 days without treatment; with antibiotics, the rash resolves after several days.

Flu-like symptoms, with fever, fatigue, headache, and muscle and joint aches may develop before or with the rash and last for a few days.

Stage two. About 20 percent of untreated people develop brain and nerve or heart-related disorders weeks or months after the bite. Some people develop a meningitis-like syndrome with fever, fatigue, and stiff neck. These symptoms also usually disappear within a few weeks.

Stage three. About half of untreated people develop recurring attacks of arthritis (joint pain) a few weeks to 2 years after the bite. Each attack can last several days to several months. The knee is the most commonly involved joint, followed by the shoulder, elbow, ankle, and wrist.

TREATMENT

1. If you develop a rash that looks like erythema migrains while in the backcountry, and you're in tick-infested territory, it is best to abort the trip and seek medical attention. The rash will help the physician diagnose Lyme disease and lead to early treatment with antibiotics. Because the blood test for

Lyme disease is inaccurate in its early stages, antibiotic treatment is commonly based on symptoms and the appearance of the typical rash. Later in the course of the disease, the test results are more accurate.

2. Lyme disease is most easily cured when antibiotics are taken early on. For stage-one disease, amoxicillin, 1 gram taken three times a day for 4 weeks, is the recommended drug of choice. An alternative is doxycycline, 200 mg twice a day for 3 days, then 100 mg twice a day for 4 weeks. A new drug that is also effective, although not yet FDA-approved for this use, is azithromycin (Zithromax®), 250 mg twice a day for only 2 weeks.

💣 Rocky Mountain Spotted Fever (RMSF)

Rocky Mountain spotted fever is caused by a microorganism called *Rickettsia rickettsii* and, like Lyme disease, is transmitted by ticks. It is most common in the states of North and South Carolina, Virginia, Maryland, Oklahoma, and the Rocky Mountain states. Each year about 800 people develop the illness in the United States, and approximately 30 people die.

SIGNS AND SYMPTOMS

• About 2 days to 2 weeks after a tick bite, victims come down with a sudden onset of fever, severe headache, upset stomach, and diffuse muscle aches.

• A rash usually appears 3 or 4 days after the onset of fever on the ankles, wrists, soles, and palms, then spreads to the trunk. Initially pink, the rash turns a deeper shade of red and eventually becomes dark bluish blotches.

• Untreated, the victim can develop heart, lung, and brain and nervous system manifestations.

TREATMENT

1. Antibiotic therapy should be initiated at the earliest suspicion of RMSF. Tetracycline (500 mg four times a day) or doxycycline (100 mg twice a day) for 14 days are both effective.

2. Without antibiotics Rocky Mountain spotted fever can be fatal so victims should seek medical attention as soon as possible.

💣 Ehrlichiosis

Erlichiosis, first discovered in 1986, is a rickettsial disease transmitted by the black-legged tick and the dog tick. It has become the most common tick-borne illness in the mid-Atlantic and south central states. Oklahoma, Missouri, and Arkansas have the highest rates of infection.

SIGNS AND SYMPTOMS

• After an average incubation period of 7 days, a high fever, headache, chills, fatigue, muscle aches, and loss of appetite typically develop.

- Some victims complain of a distorted sense of taste.
- About 20 to 40 percent of the victims develop a rash similar to Rocky Mountain spotted fever (see above). Its location is not always at the tick bite.

TREATMENT

Treatment is the same as for Rocky Mountain spotted fever (see above). Without treatment, ehrlichiosis can be fatal so victims should seek medical attention as soon as possible.

Tularemia

Several types of ticks, including the *Dermacentor* species, are known to transmit tularemia. The disease is most common in the South and Midwest, with Arkansas, Oklahoma, and Mississippi having the highest number of cases.

SIGNS AND SYMPTOMS

- Approximately 2 days after the tick bite, a red pimple or nodule forms at the site. This will eventually slough off and form an ulcer.
- At the same time, the victim usually experiences a fever and enlargement of the lymph glands.
- Some victims may also develop pneumonia.

TREATMENT

Tularemia can be treated with antibiotics, so victims should see a physician as soon as possible. Left untreated, tularemia kills about 5 percent of its victims.

Colorado (Spotted) Tick Fever

Colorado (spotted) tick fever is the most common viral illness transmitted by ticks in the United States. It is transmitted primarily by the wood tick.

SIGNS AND SYMPTOMS

- Approximately 3 to 5 days after the tick bite, the victim will develop a flu-like illness, with fever, headache, muscle aches, weakness, nausea, and chills.
- About 10 percent of victims develop a red rash.
- Some victims will feel better in 2 to 3 days and then suffer a relapse of the same symptoms 2 to 3 days later.

TREATMENT

Almost everyone gets better on their own within 2 weeks after the initial onset of symptoms. Since this is a viral illness, antibiotics are not helpful.

Babesiosis

The one major parasitic disease transmitted by ticks is babesiosis. Like Lyme disease, it is transmitted by the deer tick *(Ixodes scapularis)* and is most common in the New England states.

SIGNS AND SYMPTOMS
- Victims usually develop a flu-like illness with headache, fatigue, nausea, fever, and chills 1 to 4 weeks after the tick bite.

TREATMENT
1. Most victims recover without treatment in 1 to 2 weeks.
2. Seriously ill victims (usually people who are receiving drugs that suppress their immune system, or people who have had their spleens removed) require treatment with antibiotics. The best treatment is a combination of oral quinine 650 mg and intravenous clindamycin 600 mg every 6 hours for 3 to 5 days until the victim is no longer running a fever.

CHAPTER 19

Poison Ivy, Poison Oak, and Poison Sumac

CONTACT WITH POISON IVY, POISON OAK, or poison sumac can cause an extremely itchy rash. If you're sensitive to any one of the plants, you're likely to react to the other two because the offending substance in all three plants is the same—an oily resin known as urushiol. The risk of developing a rash after exposure to these plants increases with each exposure. Your degree of sensitivity can change drastically from one exposure to the next. You can have a minor rash one year and then experience a full-blown, head-to-toe breakout the next year.

Contrary to popular belief, urushiol is present in poison ivy and poison oak in equal amounts year round, even when the plants are only sticks or vines without leaves in the winter. In general, poison ivy grows east of the Rockies, poison oak grows west of the Rockies, and poison sumac grows best in the southeastern United States. These plants do not grow in Alaska and Hawaii, nor do they survive well above 4,000 feet, in deserts, or in rainforests.

The leaflets on poison ivy and poison oak grow in clusters of three, leading to the adage, "Leaflets three, let them be." Poison sumac leaflets grow in groups of seven to thirteen. The poison ivy vine can wind around a tree trunk or stretch across the ground. Poison oak is a low-growing shrub or woody vine, and poison sumac resembles a shrub or small tree.

PREVENTION

Barrier creams such as IvyBlock® can provide some protection by preventing the urushiol-containing plant resin from penetrating the skin. The sticky resin can stay active on clothing or shoes for many months, however, so contaminated clothing should be handled carefully and laundered immediately.

After contact with the plants, you may be able to remove the resin from the skin if you wash with soap and water within 30 minutes. Beyond 30 minutes, you can increase your chances of removing the bound resin from the skin by using a solvent like Tecnu Poison Oak-n-Ivy Cleanser®. Such solvents may be able to remove some of the oil from the skin and decrease the extent of the rash, even when used up to 8 hours after exposure.

 Backcountry Tricks
Removing Urushiol Oil from the Skin

Any solvent may help remove urushiol oil from the skin. Gasoline, paint thinner, acetone, and rubbing alcohol have all been reported to be effective. Unfortunately, these products can themselves be irritating to the skin.

SIGNS AND SYMPTOMS

- The rash may take from a few hours to days to develop. It first appears where the concentration of resin was strongest. Over time, the rash develops in a step-by-step fashion in other areas of the body where it was less concentrated, leading to the misconception that the oozing fluid from the rash spreads the rash. The rash cannot be spread by scratching after you have washed the original oil from the skin. However, scratching is still discouraged because it can produce a secondary skin infection and actually increases itching.
- The rash first appears as red, itchy bumps, followed by blisters that eventually become crusted. It can be streaky or patchy and "itches like crazy."

TREATMENT

1. If left untreated, the rash will generally clear in about 2 weeks.
2. Topical over-the-counter steroid creams (such as a 1 percent hydrocortisone cream) and calamine lotion may be useful for small patches of rash but are not very effective if you have a severe case.
3. Cool, wet compresses made with Domeboro® astringent solution may provide some relief from the itching. Or you can try soaking in a tub containing a finely ground oatmeal solution, such as Aveeno Bath Treatment.®
4. Oral antihistamines such as diphenhydramine (Benadryl®), 25 to 50 mg every 4 to 6 hours, will help relieve some of the itching, but they will also make you drowsy.
5. For a widespread rash, or one involving the face or genitals, a physician can prescribe powerful corticosteroid drugs such as prednisone, which can be taken orally or via injection. It takes about 12 hours for the drug to work, but once it does, the relief is dramatic. Side effects from a 2-week course of prednisone are generally mild and worth the benefit.

CHAPTER 20

Blisters

BLISTERS ARE ONE OF THE MOST COMMON and debilitating backcountry ailments. More backpacking trips end prematurely because of blisters than from any other cause. Blisters usually develop from friction between the shoe and the foot during walking. First a red, sore area called a "hot spot" appears. If the rubbing continues, the outer layer of the skin separates from the deeper layer and fluid fills into the space, producing a blister.

PREVENTION
Eliminate as many contributing factors as possible:
- Make sure that shoes fit properly. A shoe that is too tight causes pressure sores; one that is too loose leads to friction blisters.
- Break in new boots gradually before your trip.
- Wear a thin liner sock under a heavier one. Friction will occur between the socks instead of between the boot and the foot.
- Avoid prolonged wetness. It breaks down the skin, predisposing it to blisters. Dry feet regularly and use foot powder.
- Apply moleskin or molefoam to sensitive areas where blisters commonly occur *before* a hot spot develops.

Hot Spots
Hot spots are sore, red areas of irritation that, if allowed to progress, develop into blisters.

SIGNS AND SYMPTOMS
- The skin is red and painful at the site.
- A blister (bubble) is not yet present.

TREATMENT
1. Take a rectangular piece of moleskin (soft cotton flannel with adhesive on the back) or molefoam, which is thicker and somewhat more protective than

moleskin, and cut an oval-shaped hole in the middle (like a doughnut) the size of the hot spot (fig. 62A).

2. Center the molefoam with the hole over the affected area and secure it in place, making sure that the sticky surface is not on irritated skin (fig. 62B). This will act as a buffer against further rubbing. Applying tincture of benzoin to the skin around the blister before applying the molefoam will help hold it in place.

3. Reinforce the molefoam with tape or a piece of nonwoven adhesive knit dressing.

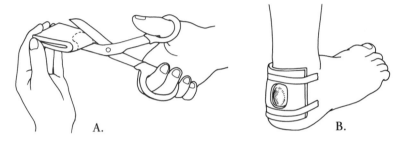

A.   B.

Figure 62A-B. Cutting a doughnut-shaped hole out of a piece of molefoam and then placing it over a blister will protect it.

💡 Backcountry Tricks
Improvising Moleskin and Molefoam

If moleskin or molefoam is not available, place a piece of tape over the hot spot. You can also improvise moleskin from the cuff of a sweatshirt or flannel shirt, and molefoam from a piece of padding from a backpack shoulder strap or hipbelt.

Blisters

If the activity which produced the hot spot continues unabated, as happens when a shoe rubs back and forth against the foot, the repeated irritation will lead to a full-blown blister.

SIGNS AND SYMPTOMS

- A bubble or pocket of fluid develops over the irritated area. The bubble can be small or quite large, and will eventually break and release clear fluid.
- There is pain and redness at the site.
- If the blister becomes infected, it will become more painful, swollen and red, and exude pus.

TREATMENT OF SMALL OR INTACT BLISTERS

1. If the blister is small, and still intact, do not puncture or drain it.
2. Place a piece of moleskin or molefoam, with a doughnut cut out slightly larger than the blister, over the site (fig. 62). It should be thick enough to keep the shoe from rubbing against the blister. This may require several layers. Applying tincture of benzoin to the skin around the blister before applying the molefoam will help hold it in place. Secure the pad with tape.

TREATMENT OF LARGE OR RUPTURED BLISTERS

1. If the bubble is intact, puncture the blister with a clean needle or safety pin at its base and massage out the fluid. The fluid contains inflammatory juices that can delay healing.
2. Use a small scissors to trim away the loose skin forming the roof of the ruptured blister.
3. Clean the area with an antiseptic towelette or soap and water.
4. Apply an antibiotic ointment (see Appendix B) or aloe vera gel, and cover with a nonadherent sterile dressing (see p. 119) or a gauze pad. Spenco 2nd Skin®, PolyMedica's Spyroflex®, Compeed's® Hydrocolloid Dressing, and Southwest Technologies' Elasto-Gel® are all excellent, albeit expensive, blister dressings.
5. Place a piece of molefoam, with a hole cut out of it slightly larger than the blister, around the site (fig. 62). Secure everything with tape or a piece of nonwoven adhesive knit dressing. Change the dressing daily or every other day. Applying tincture of benzoin to the skin around the blister before applying the molefoam will help hold it in place.
6. Inspect the wound daily for any sign of infection, such as redness around the wound, swelling, increased pain, or cloudy fluid collecting under the dressing. If infection occurs, remove the dressing to allow drainage. Consult a physician as soon as possible.

☼ Backcountry Tricks
Gluing a Blister Back in Place

If you are far from help, are without supplies to mend a blister, and must continue walking, consider this option: Drain the fluid from the blister with a sterilized pin or knife (see above) and inject a small amount of SuperGlue® or tincture of benzoin into the space that you have evacuated. Press the loose skin overlying the blister back in place, and cover the site with tape or a suitable dressing. The extreme pain this produces will only last a few minutes.

CHAPTER 21

Splinter and Fishhook Removal

SPLINTERS GENERALLY CAUSE ONLY SMALL wounds, but they can cause a variety of problems if not removed. Wood splinters left in the skin have been known to fester and cause pain for up to 7 years after becoming embedded.

Splinters

Objects that are not chemically inert, particularly wood and other organic materials such as thorns, must be removed in their entirety. Leaving part of the material in place will often lead to infection as well as pain and discomfort, especially in weight-bearing areas or near joints.

SIGNS AND SYMPTOMS

- Even if the end of the splinter is not sticking out, it may be visible just under the skin.
- The victim can often feel the foreign body when pressure is applied to the site.
- A wound that refuses to heal or continues to hurt for more than a week may harbor a splinter or other foreign body.

TREATMENT

1. *Resist* the temptation to "yank out" partially protruding wood splinters (especially rotten wood). Small fragments, which are difficult to recover, can be left behind.
2. Use a sterile needle (see p. 127), safety pin, or other sharp object to carefully trim away the skin overlying the splinter and expose the entire splinter.
3. After removing the splinter, irrigate the wound with disinfected water or sterile saline solution (see p. 116) and apply an antibiotic ointment such as Polysporin®.
4. Cover the wound with a protective dressing and bandage.
5. If a splinter is difficult to remove, do not mutilate the skin by repeated attempts, but seek medical care as soon as possible.

Backcountry Tricks
Using Glue to Remove Cactus Spines

To remove large numbers of cactus spines embedded in the skin, try using glue. Apply a thin layer of Elmer's Glue-All® to a single gauze pad and place it over the area where the spines are embedded. After the glue dries, gently peel the gauze away, pulling out the spines. Any remaining spines can be removed with tweezers or forceps.

Embedded Fishhook

For a fisherman, the only thing worse than not catching a single fish is getting impaled on the wrong end of a fishing line.

TREATMENT

Fishhooks have a barb just behind the tip and are curved so that the more force applied to the hook, the deeper it penetrates. The barb does not allow the hook to be backed out.

1. Although the classic method of advancing the barb through the skin and cutting the hook so that the remaining shank can be backed out is effective, there is an easier and less painful technique—the string-jerk method (see below).
2. After removing the hook, clean the entry point with an antiseptic towelette or soap and water.
3. *Caution:* Fishhooks embedded in the eye should be left in place and secured with tape, the eye covered with a metal patch or cup, and the victim transported to an ophthalmologist for definitive care.

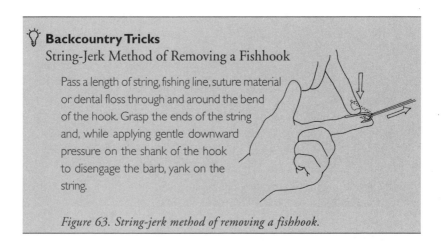 **Backcountry Tricks**
String-Jerk Method of Removing a Fishhook

Pass a length of string, fishing line, suture material or dental floss through and around the bend of the hook. Grasp the ends of the string and, while applying gentle downward pressure on the shank of the hook to disengage the barb, yank on the string.

Figure 63. String-jerk method of removing a fishhook.

CHAPTER 22

Altitude Illness

A Close Call

The young hiker, unable to walk or even to stand under his own power, lay dying in his sleeping bag in the rarefied air of Lobache, Nepal, in the heart of the Khumbu trekking region. Less than 24 hours earlier, Brad had arrived at the 16,000-foot camp eager to get a glimpse of Mount Everest Base Camp the following day. He felt tired and out of breath from the long hike up to the camp.

By nightfall he noticed a throbbing headache and had little appetite for dinner. During the night he slept poorly, awakening frequently with periods of breathlessness and the sensation that his heart was racing. When morning arrived, his head was pounding and he was nauseated. Not wanting to be a burden, Brad did not tell anyone that he was ill. He drank little that day because of the nausea and medicated his persistent headache with Tylenol® and codeine.

It wasn't until Brad didn't show up for dinner on the second night that his companions suspected that something was wrong. They found him lying in his tent, disoriented and unable to stand. The next 12 hours become an epic struggle to save his life.

Fortunately, Brad's companions recognized the ominous signs of high-altitude cerebral edema (HACE) and immediately began evacuating him to a lower altitude. With the help of headlamps and some local Sherpas, they carried Brad over treacherous terrain to the Himalayan Rescue Association clinic located at 14,000 feet in the village of Pheriche.

It was almost morning when I first saw Brad. He was partially recovered as a result of the 2,000-foot descent. I gave him Diamox® and Decadron® and placed him in a Gamow pressure bag for 4 hours. He continued to improve, and by the second day was well enough to continue descending under his own power.

Not everyone I saw at the medical clinic that year was as fortunate as Brad; there were four fatalities from high-altitude illness.

You don't have to be a high-altitude climber to feel altitude's effects. Of the more than 50 million people who travel to Colorado and Utah ski areas (8,000 to 10,000 feet or 2400 to 3400 meters) each year, 17 percent develop altitude-illness symptoms. Sixty percent of climbers on Mount Rainier (14,410 feet or 4400 meters) are afflicted with symptoms of altitude illness.

It is rare to experience altitude illness below 7,000 feet (2200 meters).

WHAT CAUSES ALTITUDE ILLNESS?

Altitude illness is a direct result of the reduced barometric pressure and the concentration of oxygen in the air at high elevations. Although the percentage of oxygen in the air stays relatively constant at 21 percent, the actual amount of oxygen you inhale with every breath decreases as barometric pressure declines. Lower pressure makes the air less dense, so your body gets fewer oxygen molecules with every breath.

The first part of the body to complain about the reduced oxygen content of the air at altitude is the brain, which uses more than 20 percent of all the oxygen consumed by the body. In order to compensate for the decreased oxygen, blood vessels supplying the brain dilate to allow more blood—and thus more oxygen—to flow to the head. The engorged brain begins to swell, resulting in one of the first and most common symptoms of altitude illness: a headache. Progressive swelling of the brain can eventually lead to high-altitude cerebral edema (HACE), which if untreated, can lead to unconsciousness, coma, and death.

The lungs, which oxygenate all the body's blood, also require more blood flow when the air gets thin. Increased blood flow to the lungs causes increased pressure in the blood vessels, which can cause fluid to leak out of the blood vessels and into the air spaces, producing high-altitude pulmonary edema (HAPE). The obstructive fluid makes it difficult for the oxygen in the air to diffuse into the blood system, worsening the body's oxygen debt.

PREVENTION

Graded ascent is the surest and safest method of preventing altitude illness. Avoid abrupt ascent to sleeping altitudes greater than 10,000 feet (3,000 meters), and average no more than 1,000 feet (300 meters) of elevation gain per day above 10,000 feet. Day trips to a higher altitude, with a return to lower altitude for sleep, will aid acclimatization. Eat foods that are high in carbohydrates and low in fat.

Some individuals are inherently more susceptible to altitude illness and will get sick despite a graded and slow ascent. Being in good physical condition does not impart protection from altitude illness. In fact, well-conditioned athletes may sometimes be more susceptible to altitude illness because they are conditioned not to hyperventilate when their bodies are low on oxygen, and an increased respiratory rate is one of the most important acclimatizing adaptations to high altitude (see below).

Acetazolamide (Diamox®) is a prescription medication that may help prevent altitude illness when used in conjunction with graded ascent. Diamox® works by increasing the respiratory rate, which is especially beneficial while you're asleep and naturally breathing less. It is also a diuretic and may predispose you to dehydration, so drink lots of fluids, and be prepared for the inconvenience of frequent urination. The recommended preventative dose is 125 mg the morning before you arrive at altitude, again that evening, and then twice a day while you are ascending. Continue taking Diamox® for at least 48 hours after reaching your maximum altitude.

Caution: Before using Diamox®, consult a physician. It can cause an allergic reaction in certain individuals and produce numbness and tingling in the hands and feet. Diamox® will also ruin the taste of beer, cola, and other carbonated beverages.

 Backcountry Tricks
Power Breathing

Anything that will increase the amount of oxygen getting into the blood at high altitude is of benefit. Taking deeper breaths and exhaling against pursed lips to create some back pressure may open up more lung sacs and produce greater oxygenation of the blood. This technique is frequently used by Mount Rainier climbing guides.

The Golden Rules of Altitude Illness

1. Above 8,000 feet (2400 meters), headache, nausea, shortness of breath, and vomiting should be considered to be altitude illness until proven otherwise.
2. No one with mild symptoms of altitude illness should ascend any higher until the symptoms have resolved.
3. Anyone with worsening symptoms or severe symptoms of altitude illness should descend immediately to a lower altitude.

Mild Altitude Illness (Acute Mountain Sickness)

Mild altitude illness, known as acute mountain sickness (AMS), is common in travelers who ascend rapidly to altitudes above 8,000 feet (2400 meters). Children are generally more susceptible than are adults.

SIGNS AND SYMPTOMS

- The typical sufferer experiences a headache, difficulty sleeping, loss of appetite, and nausea.
- Swelling of the face and hands may be an early sign.
- Symptoms usually begin on the second day after reaching a high elevation.
- AMS sufferers commonly manifest an alteration of the normal sleeping pattern know as periodic, or Cheyne-Stokes, breathing. Sleep is fitful, with frequent awakenings, and breathing is irregular, with periods of rapid breathing alternating with periods of no breathing.

TREATMENT

1. When mild symptoms develop, it is a signal that the victim should not go any higher in altitude until the symptoms have completely resolved. Watch the victim closely for progression of illness to HAPE or HACE (see below). Usually, within 1 or 2 days, the victim will feel better and can then travel to higher altitudes with caution. Symptoms will improve more rapidly simply by going down a few thousand feet.
2. Administer acetaminophen (Tylenol®), 650 to 1000 mg every 4 to 6 hours or ibuprofen (Motrin®), 600 mg every 8 hours with food, for headache.
3. Consider administering acetazolamide (Diamox®) (see above), at a treatment dose of 250 mg twice a day.
4. Minimize exertion.
5. Avoid sleeping pills, which can reduce the respiratory rate even further.

☀ Severe Altitude Illness

Progression of the victim's symptoms, despite rest at the same altitude, or the loss of coordination, demand immediate descent to a lower altitude (about 2,000 to 3,000 feet or 900 meters lower). Tragedy has too often occurred when parties elected to wait until morning to begin descent. A victim who might have been able to walk down under his own power with the aid of a headlamp can easily become a litter case in just 12 hours.

The single most useful sign for recognizing the progression of altitude illness from mild to severe is *loss of coordination*. The victim tends to stagger, has trouble with balance, and is unable to walk a straight line heel-to-toe, as if he were drunk.

If the victim develops any signs or symptoms of HAPE or HACE (see below), he should descend immediately. Never allow a victim to descend by himself. Always have a healthy person accompany the victim.

☀WHEN TO WORRY
High-Altitude Cerebral Edema (HACE)

High Altitude Cerebral Edema refers to a disorder of brain swelling at high altitude that leads to a headache, vomiting, and alteration of mental status and coordination. In severe cases it can produce unconsciousness, coma, and death.

Note: A victim may have signs and symptoms of both HACE and HAPE (see below) simultaneously.

SIGNS AND SYMPTOMS

A victim of HACE may have one or more of the following symptoms:

- Severe headache unrelieved by acetaminophen (Tylenol®) or ibuprofen (Motrin®).
- Vomiting.
- Loss of coordination.
- Severe fatigue.
- Confusion, inappropriate behavior, hallucinations, stupor, or coma.
- Transient blindness, partial paralysis, or loss of sensation on one side of the body may occur.
- Seizures.

TREATMENT

1. **Immediate descent** of at least 3,000 feet (900 meters), or until the victim shows signs of considerable improvement. Do not wait to see if the victim gets worse or for the condition to get better. *Waiting could prove to be fatal.*
2. Administer acetazolamide (Diamox®), 250 mg twice a day.
3. Administer dexamethasone (Decadron®), 8 mg followed by 4 mg every 6 hours.
4. Administer oxygen if available.
5. When descent is not immediately possible, placing the victim in a portable hyperbaric chamber called a Gamow Bag® may be helpful in reversing the effects of HACE or HAPE. When zippered shut with the victim inside, this nylon bag is pressurized with the use of a foot pump, resulting in a significant decrease in altitude for the victim. The greater pressure inside the bag allows more oxygen to be delivered to the victim's blood. The bag takes approximately 2 minutes to inflate and is very labor-intensive, requiring 10 to 15 pumps per minute to maintain pressure and flush out carbon dioxide.
6. The victim will usually improve after about 1 hour in the bag for HACE

(longer—sometimes up to 4 hours—for HAPE) but may need to stay in the bag for several hours, depending on the severity of his condition. The Gamow Bag® should not be used as a substitute for descent; it should be used when descent is not possible because of darkness, injury, or if there are not enough rescuers to carry the victim to a lower altitude.

💣 WHEN TO WORRY
High-Altitude Pulmonary Edema (HAPE)

High-altitude pulmonary edema (HAPE) usually begins within the first 2 to 4 days of ascent to higher altitudes, most commonly on the second night. Although HAPE is the most common cause of death related to high altitude, if recognized early and treated properly, it is easily and completely reversed.

Note: A victim may have signs and symptoms of both HACE (see above) and HAPE simultaneously.

SIGNS AND SYMPTOMS

A victim of HAPE may have one or more of the following symptoms:

- Initially the victim will notice marked breathlessness with minor exertion and develop a dry, hacking cough.
- As greater amounts of fluid accumulate in the lungs, the victim develops increasing shortness of breath, even while resting, and a cough that produces frothy, often blood-tinged, sputum.
- The victim looks anxious, is restless, and has a rapid, bounding pulse.
- Cyanosis (a bluish color of the lips and nails indicating poor oxygenation of the blood) may be present.

TREATMENT

1. **Immediate descent** of at least 3,000 feet (900 meters), or until the victim shows signs of considerable improvement is the only sure treatment. Do not wait to see if the victim gets worse or for the condition to get better. *Waiting could prove to be fatal.*
2. Administer oxygen if available.
3. Administer nifedipine (Procardia®), 10 to 20 mg every 8 hours.
4. The use of a Gamow Bag® (see above) may be beneficial when the victim cannot be immediately evacuated to a lower altitude.

Peripheral Edema (Swelling)

Swelling of the face, hands, and feet may occur after 2 to 6 days at high altitude. Women are more commonly affected than men. The swelling usually persists for 1 to 3 days after return to lower altitude, and resolves spontaneously without treatment.

SIGNS AND SYMPTOMS

- Swelling (puffiness) of the eyelids, face, hands, feet, and ankles.
- Swelling is usually worse in the morning.
- The victim may notice a decreased urge to urinate.

TREATMENT

1. Someone with peripheral edema is probably more susceptible to altitude illness and should be monitored closely for the development of signs and symptoms of AMS, HACE, or HAPE.
2. The use of potent diuretics such as Furosemide (Lasix®) to decrease the edema is not recommended as it can lead to problems with dehydration.
3. Diamox®, which is a weak diuretic, may be helpful (125 mg twice a day).

High-Altitude Pharyngitis and Bronchitis

Due to rapid breathing of cold, dry air at altitude, the mucous membranes lining the throat and windpipe dry out and become irritated.

SIGNS AND SYMPTOMS

- Sore throat.
- Hacking cough.
- Dehydration.
- Congestion.

TREATMENT

1. Drink copious amounts of fluids.
2. Afrin® or Neosynephrine® nasal sprays may help reduce nasal congestion.
3. Lozenges or hard candies will help the sore throat.
4. Carefully inhaling steam from a pot of boiling water may be beneficial.

CHAPTER 23

Hypothermia

HYPOTHERMIA IS AN ABNORMALLY LOW body-core temperature resulting from exposure to a cold environment. Core temperature typically refers to a temperature taken rectally. Normal core (rectal) temperature is 99 degrees Fahrenheit, whereas normal oral temperature is 98.6 degrees. Core temperature down to 90 degrees is considered mild to moderate hypothermia. Core temperatures below 90 degrees indicate profound or severe hypothermia.

There is no exact core temperature at which one perishes from hypothermia. When the body core temperature falls below 83 degrees, the heart becomes very irritable and is prone to lethal irregularities (arrhythmias) such as ventricular fibrillation. During the infamous Dachau prison camp experiments, Nazi scientists documented death to occur at a body core temperature of around 72 to 77 degrees. The lowest recorded core temperature in a surviving adult is 60.8 degrees. For a child it is 57 degrees.

Although very few people freeze to death in the backcountry, fatal accidents and injuries resulting from hypothermia-induced poor judgment and incoordination are all too common.

PREVENTION

Heat is lost from the body in four general ways, each of which can be prevented or minimized by simple precautions:

1. *Radiation* is the direct loss of heat from a warm body to a cooler environment. Your head and neck alone can account for 50 percent of your total body heat loss. Protective clothing, including a hat and scarf, will help prevent radiant heat loss.

2. *Conduction* is heat loss through direct physical contact between the body and a cooler surface. Insulating yourself from the ground will help prevent this type of heat loss.

3. *Convection* is heat loss by air movement circulating around the body and depends on the velocity of the wind (wind chill factor). Windproof clothing

and shelter will help reduce this type of heat loss. In a survival situation, wrapping a garbage bag around yourself or even using your pack as a bivy sac can help protect you from wind chill.

4. *Evaporation* is heat loss through sweat drying on your skin. Using a vapor barrier liner under your clothing minimizes this type of heat loss. Heat is also lost by breathing cold, dry air. Breathing through a scarf or face mask can reduce this type of heat loss.

How Your Body Recognizes and Reacts to Being Cold

Your perception of whether you are cold or warm depends more on your skin temperature than on your core temperature. Your body's thermostat is in your skin, not your core or brain. Even when your core temperature is above normal, if your skin is cold you will "feel" cold and begin shivering (an involuntary condition in which your muscles contract rapidly to generate additional body heat). And if your core temperature is low but your skin is warm, you will "feel" warm, and will not shiver despite being hypothermic.

If you warm your skin without providing any heat to the core, you extinguish the drive to shiver and thus produce less heat. If, for example, a hypothermic victim drinks some whiskey or gin, the alcohol will cause the blood vessels on the skin to dilate; the victim will feel warmer, stop shivering, and become even more hypothermic.

Mild Hypothermia

When the body core temperature drops below 95 degrees Fahrenheit, a victim enters the zone of mild hypothermia.

SIGNS AND SYMPTOMS
- The victim feels cold, and shivering reaches its maximum level.
- The victim maintains a normal level of consciousness, is alert, and has normal or only slightly impaired coordination.
- When the core temperature drops below 93 degrees, the victim develops apathy, amnesia, slurred speech, and poor judgment.

TREATMENT
1. Remove the victim from the cold environment and get him into shelter.
2. Replace any wet clothing with dry, insulated garments.
3. Give the victim warm food and lots of sugary hot fluids (like JELL-O®) to drink. An average-size person will need to consume about 60 kilocalories' worth of a hot beverage to elevate his core temperature 1 degree Fahrenheit.

Since 1 quart of hot JELL-O® at 140 degrees provides about 30 kilocalories, a victim would have to consume 2 quarts to raise his temperature 1 degree. The sugar content of the fluid is probably more important, however, as it will provide added fuel for the victim's furnace so that he can generate his own internal heat.

4. You can slow heat loss by wrapping the victim in a sleeping bag, plastic bag, or tarp. Huddling together with the victim in a sleeping bag will reduce heat loss.

5. Resist the urge to use hot-water bottles or heat packs as they can turn off the shivering mechanism and, by themselves, add very little heat to the body core. Instead, bring water to a boil and have the victim inhale the steam, or build a fire.

 Backcountry Tricks
Fast Fuel for Your Body's Furnace

Glutose Paste®, an oral glucose gel containing concentrated sugar for treating hypoglycemia and insulin reactions in diabetics, is an excellent item to carry in your pocket when you're out in the cold. The concentrated sugar in the tube is absorbed into the blood rapidly from the stomach and provides a powerful source of fuel for your body to generate heat.

WHEN TO WORRY
Profound Hypothermia

When the body core temperature drops below 90 degrees Fahrenheit, a victim crosses the boundary into profound hypothermia, and is in serious trouble.

SIGNS AND SYMPTOMS

- The victim becomes weak and lethargic.
- The victim has an altered mental state (disorientation, confusion, combative or irrational behavior, or coma).
- The victim is uncoordinated.
- At a body core temperature below 88 degrees, the victim will stop shivering.
- At a core temperature below 86 degrees, the victim's heart pumps less than two-thirds the normal amount of blood. Pulse and respirations will be half of normal.

- At a core temperature below 83 degrees, the heart is very irritable and unstable and prone to developing irregularities such as ventricular fibrillation. The victim is in danger of sudden cardiac arrest. Rough handling of the victim increases the potential for cardiac arrest.

TREATMENT

First-aid treatment in the backcountry is aimed at stabilizing the victim and preventing any further cooling.

1. Handle the victim very gently. Rough handling may cause the victim's heart to fail.
2. Place the victim in a sleeping bag, or place blankets or clothing underneath and on top of him. Any heat that you can provide will probably not rewarm the victim but will help prevent further cooling.
3. A victim with a significantly altered mental state should not be allowed to eat or drink because of the potential for choking and vomiting.
4. Rewarming is best done in a hospital, because of the potential complications associated with profound hypothermia. Professional assistance is usually needed to evacuate a profoundly hypothermic victim (see Appendix C).

Caution: First-aid management of hypothermic victims should not be based solely on measurements of body temperature because obtaining an accurate temperature in the field can be difficult. Body temperature is only one consideration along with other observations and signs (such as an altered mental state) in guiding the decisions about appropriate treatment.

It may be difficult to distinguish between someone who is profoundly hypothermic and someone who is dead. The profoundly hypothermic person may have a pulse and respirations that are barely detectable. Double-check carefully, feeling for the carotid pulse (see fig. 12) for at least 1 full minute in a hypothermic victim, since the heart rate may be very slow. Place a cold glass surface next to the victim's mouth to see if it fogs up.

WHEN TO PERFORM CARDIOPULMONARY RESUSCITATION (CPR)

If the victim is breathing or has any pulse, no matter how slow, do not initiate CPR, as this may cause the heart to stop completely. If there is no sign of a pulse or breathing after 1 minute, what to do next depends on your situation:

1. If you are alone or with only one other person, cover the victim and place him in a protected shelter (place insulation on top of and underneath him). Both rescuers should go for help and stay together for safety.
2. If there are multiple rescuers, and it is safe to stay with the victim, begin CPR (see p. 26). Chest compressions should be done at one-half the normal rate. At least two people should go for help and stay together for safety.

3. If the victim can be easily transported out of the backcountry in an improvised stretcher (see pp. 228–229), the rescuers may elect to do this while
performing CPR during the transport as best as possible.

Caution: Never assume that a profoundly hypothermic victim is dead until
his body has been warmed and there are still no signs of life. Rarely, a victim
who is without detectable signs of life, and is therefore presumed to be dead,
will recover when rewarmed.

 Backcountry Tricks
"Sobriety" Test for Hypothermia

An excellent test to determine if someone is developing profound hypothermia is to have the person walk a straight line, heel-to-toe, as in a sobriety
test. If the person cannot perform this task and is not intoxicated, it suggests
the progression from mild to profound hypothermia.

Characteristics Associated with Body Core Temperatures

Body Core Temperature	Characteristics•
99° F	Normal rectal temperature.
98.6° F	Normal oral temperature.
95° F	Maximum shivering.
93° F	Poor judgment, slower movement.
91.5° F	Clumsy movements, apathy.
88° F	Shivering stops, stupor, altered level of consciousness.
83°–86° F	Heart is irritable and prone to arrhythmias.
80° F	Voluntary motion ceases, pupils not reactive to light.
72°–77° F	Maximum risk of cardiac arrest.

•General guidelines only—marked variations may occur.

CHAPTER 24

Cold-Induced Injuries

COLD-INDUCED INJURIES (frostbite and immersion foot) occur in cold and windy weather conditions. Even if the temperature outdoors is not very cold, high winds can reduce the effective temperature to a dangerously low level. The chilling effect of air at 20 degrees Fahrenheit moving at 40 miles an hour is the same as 20-below-zero air on a still day.

PREVENTION

On long trips it is important to drink often to prevent dehydration and to eat often to provide fuel for your body to generate heat. If the body is cold and dehydrated, it will shunt blood away from the skin, which can predispose one to cold-induced injuries.

Other things that predispose one to cold-induced injuries and that should be avoided include smoking, tight restrictive clothing and shoes, and contact of bare flesh with cold metal or moisture. Avoid overexertion and excessive perspiration. Individuals with diabetes or poor circulation are more likely to suffer cold-induced injuries.

 Backcountry Tricks
Windmilling for Warmth

If you feel your fingers getting numb from the cold, swing your arms around in a circle like a windmill for a few minutes. Windmilling increases blood flow to the hands and fingers and may delay the onset of frostbite.

Wind (wind chill factor) original information on the importance of windchill comes from the work of C. F. Passel and P. A. Siple while working in Antarctica during the winter of 1941. They developed a formula that expressed heat loss as a function of wind speed and air temperatures.

Wind Speed MPH	Temperature (°F) — Equivalent Chill Temperature																					
	50	40	35	30	25	20	15	10	5	0	-5	-10	-15	-20	-25	-30	-35	-40	-45	-50	-55	-60
Calm	50	40	35	30	25	20	15	10	5	0	-5	-10	-15	-20	-25	-30	-35	-40	-45	-50	-55	-60
5	48	37	33	27	21	16	12	6	1	-5	-11	-15	-20	-26	-31	-36	-41	-47	-52	-57	-65	-70
10	40	28	21	16	9	4	-2	-9	-15	-24	-27	-33	-38	-46	-52	-58	-64	-70	-75	-83	-90	-95
15	36	22	16	9	1	-5	-11	-18	-25	-32	-40	-45	-51	-58	-65	-72	-77	-85	-90	-99	-105	-110
20	32	18	12	4	-4	-10	-17	-25	-32	-39	-46	-53	-60	-67	-75	-82	-89	-96	-102	-110	-115	-120
25	30	16	7	0	-7	-15	-22	-29	-37	-44	-52	-59	-67	-74	-83	-88	-96	-104	-111	-118	-125	-135
30	28	13	5	-2	-11	-18	-26	-33	-41	-48	-56	-63	-70	-79	-87	-94	-101	-109	-115	-125	-130	-140
35	27	11	3	-4	-13	-20	-27	-35	-43	-51	-60	-67	-72	-82	-90	-98	-105	-113	-120	-129	-135	-146
40	26	10	1	-6	-15	-21	-29	-37	-45	-53	-62	-69	-76	-85	-94	-100	-107	-115	-125	-132	-140	-150
above 40	little additional effect																					

Danger of Freezing Exposed Flesh if Dry and Properly Clothed: Little Danger Great Extreme

Frostnip

Frostnip (also called superficial frostbite) is early cold injury to the skin and does not usually lead to permanent damage if the skin is rewarmed immediately. It may progress to deeper frostbite if left untreated.

SIGNS AND SYMPTOMS

- Frostnip is characterized by numbness of the involved area. Common locations are the fingers, toes, nose, and ear lobes.
- The affected part will initially appear red and then turn pale or whitish.
- Frostnipped parts are still soft to the touch.

TREATMENT

1. Frostnipped areas should be rewarmed immediately to prevent the progression to frostbite. Place your fingers in your own armpit or groin and leave them there until they are warm and no longer numb. Place your bared feet onto the warm stomach of a companion.
2. Chemical heat packs are also beneficial, but take care not to burn the skin.

☀ Frostbite

Frostbite is freezing of the skin and usually indicates that some degree of permanent damage has occurred. Appropriate field care is critical to minimize the amount of tissue loss.

SIGNS AND SYMPTOMS

- Frostbite is recognized by skin that is white and waxy in appearance.
- The affected part feels hard to the touch, like a piece of wood or frozen piece of meat.
- The frostbitten part may not be painful until it is rewarmed.

TREATMENT

1. The best treatment for frostbite is rapid rewarming in warm water (between 104 and 106 degrees Fahrenheit) as soon as the victim can be maintained in a warm environment. Rapid rewarming is preferable to slow rewarming, since the damage to tissue occurs during the actual freezing and thawing phases. If possible, avoid rewarming the frostbitten area if there is a danger of refreezing. Walking to shelter on frozen feet is much less damaging than walking on feet that have been thawed. Allowing the feet to refreeze again after thawing is the worst possible scenario.
2. Rapidly rewarm frozen extremities in water at a temperature of 104 to 106 degrees Fahrenheit. Circulate the water to keep the involved part in contact

with the warmest water, and avoid rubbing or massaging the skin. Keep checking the water temperature, as it will cool quickly, and add more hot water if needed. Remove the extremity from the water before adding more hot water.

3. Thawing in warm water usually requires 30 to 45 minutes of immersion and can be very painful. If pain medication is available, a dose may be given to the victim before beginning (see Appendix B). Thawing is complete when the paleness has turned to a pink or red color and the skin is soft.

4. After thawing, the involved part will be very sensitive to further injury and should be protected. Applying a thin layer of aloe vera gel to the skin will promote healing.

5. When frostbite is rewarmed, fluid-filled blisters (blebs) may form. If this occurs, do not pop the blisters. If blisters rupture spontaneously, remove the loose skin overlying the blister and apply aloe vera gel or antibiotic ointment.

6. Place small sterile gauze pads between toes or fingers, cover the injury with a nonadherent sterile dressing (see p. 119), and loosely wrap the extremity with a bulky bandage.

7. To relieve pain and minimize tissue loss, administer ibuprofen (Motrin®), 600 to 800 mg every 12 hours, or aspirin, 650 mg every 6 hours.

8. Elevate and splint (see p. 77) the affected part.

9. The depth and degree of the frozen tissue cannot be readily ascertained by looking at the part. Even terrible-looking limbs often recover if treated well, so reassure the victim and seek professional medical care as soon as possible.

WHAT NOT TO DO

1. Do not rub the affected part with snow. In fact, do not massage, rub, or touch the frozen part at all.

2. Be careful not to use water that is hotter than 106 degrees Fahrenheit, since a burn injury may result. Hot packs and heating pads should be used with caution, as they also increase the risk of burn injury.

3. The victim should not smoke or chew tobacco. The nicotine from one cigarette reduces blood flow to the skin, fingers, and toes by at least 10 percent.

4. Do not thaw the frozen extremity in front of a fire or stove.

5. Do not let the thawed extremity refreeze.

6. Walking on frostbitten feet or using frostbitten fingers will cause further injury and should be avoided when possible.

Immersion Foot (Trenchfoot)

Trenchfoot occurs in response to exposure to nonfreezing cold and wet conditions over a number of days, leading to damage of blood vessels, nerves, skin, and sometimes muscle, without direct freezing of tissues.

SIGNS AND SYMPTOMS

- Numbness and/or a painful pins-and-needles sensation may be experienced in the feet.
- During the first few hours to days, the feet become very red and swollen and then mottled with dark burgundy-to-blue splotches.
- The feet can become extremely painful after rewarming and very sensitive to cold and touching.

TREATMENT

Keep the affected area dry and warm and treat in a manner identical for frostbite (see above), with the exception that rapid rewarming (thawing) is not necessary.

CHAPTER 25

Heat-Related Illnesses

Heat emergencies encompass a spectrum of illnesses, ranging from minor reactions such as muscle cramps to heat stroke, a life-threatening emergency. Although heat illness is readily preventable, thousands of people continue to suffer and die of heat each year. Heat stroke is the second leading cause of death in athletes.

There are some days when it is definitely better to rest in the shade or camp indoors next to the air conditioner. The potential for developing heat illness is greatest in an environment that is both hot and humid. When the outside temperature exceeds 95 degrees Fahrenheit, evaporation of sweat from the body's surface is the only mechanism left to dissipate heat. If the humidity level then exceeds 80 percent, the body's ability to lose heat (from evaporation) declines dramatically, and the risk of developing heat illness soars. Sweat that merely drips from the skin and is not evaporated only contributes to dehydration without providing any cooling benefit.

The environment isn't the only thing that can make you hot. Your body generates 2,000 to 5,000 kilocalories a day all by itself, just through normal metabolic functions. If you did not have effective mechanisms for dissipating heat, basal metabolism alone would raise your temperature 1.5 degrees Fahrenheit every hour. When you carry a heavy pack in hot temperatures, your internal heat production can increase five to tenfold.

PREVENTION

1. **Keep yourself well hydrated.** Dehydration is the most important contributing factor leading to heat illness. When you're overheated, the superficial blood vessels dilate, channeling more blood to your skin surface where your body heat can be given off by radiation to the "cooler" air. If you're dehydrated, the blood vessels in the skin will constrict because

there is not enough blood volume to keep them expanded. The amount of heat that you can radiate into the environment will then be greatly reduced. More important, dehydration limits the ability of the body to sweat and evaporate heat.

Unfortunately, our body's dehydration sensor is not very sensitive. It waits until we're already 2 to 5 percent dehydrated before sounding the thirst alarm, and then shuts off prematurely after we have replaced only two-thirds of the fluid deficit. Loss of only 1 more liter of water through sweating after you become thirsty produces severe dehydration, reduces your physical capacity significantly, and increases your risk of developing heat illness. The best way to tell if you're hydrated is the urine-color gauge: clear to pale yellow urine indicates that a you are drinking enough fluids; dark yellow urine indicates dehydration. (*Note:* Some vitamins and medications can also turn urine a yellow-orange color.)

During exercise, you can easily sweat away 1 to 2 liters of water per hour. Keeping yourself hydrated requires a continual, conscious effort. Carry your water bottle where it is easily accessible, and drink at least ½ liter every 20 minutes while hiking. As a general rule of thumb, in a hot environment, you should carry 1 gallon of water for every 20 miles walked at night and 2 gallons for every 20 miles walked during the day.

The colder and more tasty the beverage is, the more likely you will want to drink. Colder fluids are also more easily absorbed from the stomach. Wrap the bottle in an article of clothing to help keep it cool, and add a powdered sports drink mix after disinfecting the water. Your body can absorb a carbohydrate-containing beverage up to 30 percent faster than plain water. A 6 or 7 percent carbohydrate concentration, such as diluted Gatorade® (⅓ to ½ strength), is ideal. Higher carbohydrate concentrations should be avoided because they can produce stomach cramps and delay absorption.

Salt lost in sweating can usually be replaced by a normal diet. However, an unacclimatized individual working in the heat for 8 hours a day can develop a salt deficit and electrolyte imbalance unless a small amount of salt is added to drinking water. The ideal concentration is a 0.1 percent salt solution, which can be prepared by dissolving two 10-grain salt tablets or ¼ teaspoon of table salt in 1 liter of water (crush the tablets first before attempting to dissolve them). *Salt tablets should not be eaten by themselves—they irritate the stomach, produce vomiting, and do not treat the dehydration that is also present.*

To Avoid Dehydration

Drink fluids even when you are not thirsty!

2. **Hike in the early morning and late afternoon** when the sun is low and the heat is less intense.
3. **Avoid medications and drugs that predispose you to heat illness.** Examples include:
    a. Antihistamines found in many cold and allergy preparations decrease the rate of sweating.
    b. Antihypertension drugs such as beta-blockers, ace inhibitors, and diuretics can predispose you to heat illness.
    c. Amphetamines, PCP, and cocaine can all cause heat illness by increasing metabolic heat production.
4. **Acclimatize.** Allow yourself adequate time to acclimatize before exercising for prolonged periods in the heat. It takes about 10 days to become acclimatized to a hot environment. During this time, you will need to do about 2 hours of exercise each day. With acclimatization, your body becomes more efficient at cooling itself and you are less likely to suffer heat illness. You begin sweating earlier, and the amount of sweat you can produce may double or quadruple. There is less salt lost in the sweat, and so electrolytes are conserved.
5. **Wear lightweight, light-colored, and loose-fitting clothes.** Light colors reflect the heat more than dark colors, and loose-fitting clothes allow more ventilation.
6. **Get plenty of rest.** A U.S. Army study found that lack of sleep and fatigue predispose people to heat illness.
7. **Be aware of the level of environmental heat stress and adjust your activity accordingly.** The best indicator of environmental heat stress is the wet-bulb globe temperature index (WBGT) (see sidebar). The WBGT measures three forms of heat load:
    a. Dry-air temperature (measured by a regular thermometer).
    b. The effect of humidity on the temperature (measured by wet-bulb thermometer).
    c. The effect of radiant heat from the sun (measured by a globe thermometer).

Backcountry Tricks
Measuring Environmental Heat Stress

Since the wet-bulb globe temperature index is complex, and since 70 percent of the value is derived from the wet-bulb thermometer (WBT), a simple way to measure environmental heat stress in the field is with a sling psychrometer.

The sling psychrometer is made up of a wet-bulb thermometer (WBT) with a wick surrounding the bulb, attached to an aluminum frame with a hinged handle. After the wick is moistened, the psychrometer is slung over the head for approximately 2 minutes. Air passing over the wetted thermometer bulb cools the bulb in inverse proportion to the humidity. The WBT reading can then be used as an indicator of heat stress and as a guide for recommended activity levels (see sidebar).

Wet-Bulb Temperature and Recommended Activity Levels
Wet-Bulb Globe Temperature (WBGT) Recommendations

°C	°F	
15.5	60	No precautions necessary
16.2–21	61–70	No precautions necessary provided adequate hydration maintained
22–24	71–75	*Unacclimatized:* Curtail exercise; *Acclimatized:* Exercise with caution. Take rest periods and water breaks every 20 to 30 minutes
24.5–26	76–80	*Unacclimatized:* Avoid hiking or sports or sun exposure; *Acclimatized:* Heavy to moderate exercise with caution
27–30	81–85	Limited brief exercise for acclimatized fit individuals only
31	88	Avoid exercise and sun exposure

Heat Edema

Swelling of the hands, feet, and ankles is common during the first few days in a hot environment. It is more common in the elderly.

SIGNS AND SYMPTOMS

- Swelling or puffiness in the hands, feet, and ankles.
- Rings may become tight, and difficult to remove.

TREATMENT

1. The swelling usually goes away by itself in a few days and does not require any treatment.
2. Remove any constrictive rings or other jewelry.

Prickly Heat (Miliaria Rubra)

Miliaria rubra is a heat rash caused by plugging of sweat glands in the skin.

SIGNS AND SYMPTOMS

- An itchy red, bumpy rash develops on areas of the skin kept wet from sweating.

TREATMENT

1. Cool and dry the involved skin and avoid conditions that may induce sweating.
2. Taking an antihistamine such as diphenhydramine (Benadryl®), 25 to 50 mg every 4 to 6 hours, may help relieve itching.

Heat Cramps

Heat cramps are intensely painful muscle spasms that typically occur in heavily exercised muscles.

SIGNS AND SYMPTOMS

- The victim complains of severe cramping of the muscles in the calf, thigh, hands, or abdomen.
- Cramping often begins after exertion has ended and the person is resting.

TREATMENT

1. Drink plenty of fluids containing small amounts of salt (see above). Salt tablets taken by themselves are not advised.
2. Rest in a cool environment, and apply gentle, steady pressure to the cramped muscle.

Heat Syncope

When a person stands for a long time without moving, blood pools in the legs, instead of returning to the heart. Standing in a hot environment also causes blood vessels on the surface of the skin to dilate, taking more blood away from the heart, which means there is less blood returning to the brain. The combined effect can cause someone to faint from insufficient blood flow to the brain.

SIGNS AND SYMPTOMS
- The victim becomes light-headed and dizzy and often faints or has to lie down to avoid passing out.

TREATMENT
1. Keep the victim lying in a horizontal position with the legs elevated until his symptoms have completely resolved.
2. Cool the skin with water, or place cool packs next to the armpits, neck, or groin.
3. Give the victim cool fluids to drink.

Heat Exhaustion

Heat exhaustion is the most commonly encountered form of heat illness. Heat exhaustion that is not treated can progress to full-blown heat stroke (see below).

SIGNS AND SYMPTOMS
- Flu-like symptoms (malaise, headache, weakness, nausea, and loss of appetite) are almost always present.
- Vomiting can occur.
- The victim may feel dizzy when standing up from a sitting or lying position.
- The victim's core temperature may be normal or moderately elevated (less than 104 degrees Fahrenheit).
- The victim is usually sweating and always has a normal mental state.

TREATMENT
1. Have the victim stop all exertion and move to a cool and shaded environment.
2. Remove any restrictive clothing.
3. Have the victim drink plenty of fluids containing small amounts of salt (see above).
4. Ice or cold packs should be placed alongside the neck, chest wall, under the armpits, and in the groin. *(Caution: Do not place ice directly against the skin for prolonged periods.)* Fanning while splashing the skin with tepid water, or soaking the victim in cool water, are other cooling methods.

☀WHEN TO WORRY
Heat Stroke

When the body's cooling system breaks down completely, the result is heat stroke, which has a mortality rate of 80 percent when left untreated. *This is a true medical emergency.* The difference between heat stroke and heat exhaustion is that victims with heat stroke have abnormal changes in their mental state and neurological functions.

SIGNS AND SYMPTOMS

- The victim's core temperature (measured with a rectal thermometer) is always very high (usually above 105 to 106 degrees Fahrenheit).
- Mental state is altered: the victim may be confused or disoriented, act in a bizarre manner, lose coordination (be unable to walk a straight line), or develop seizures or coma.
- The heart rate is usually rapid (greater than 100 beats per minute), blood pressure is low (it may be difficult to feel a pulse in the wrist), and breathing is rapid (more than 20 breaths per minute).
- The victim may have stopped sweating, but more commonly *sweating is still present.*
- Dry, hot skin is a very late finding and may not occur in some victims. Anyone who has a temperature above 105 degrees Fahrenheit and an altered mental state should be considered to have heat stroke, whether or not they are still sweating.

TREATMENT

1. Cool the victim as quickly as possible. Place ice or cold packs alongside the neck, chest wall, under the armpits, and in the groin. *(Caution: Do not place ice directly against the skin for prolonged periods.)* Wet the victim's skin with tepid water, and fan him rapidly to facilitate evaporative cooling. Immerse the victim carefully in cool water if available.
2. Do not give the victim anything to drink because of the risk of vomiting and aspiration.
3. Acetaminophen (Tylenol®) and aspirin are not helpful in heat stroke and should not be given.
4. Treat for shock (see p. 33).
5. Evacuate the victim as soon as possible to the closest medical facility (see Appendix C). Continue to cool the victim along the way until his temperature falls to 100 or 101 degrees Fahrenheit.
6. Recheck the victim's temperature at least every 30 minutes.

ᗐ Backcountry Tricks
Cooling a Victim of Heat Stroke

Placing ice or cold packs alongside the neck, chest wall, under the armpits, and in the groin can cool a victim of heat stroke just as fast as placing his entire body in a tub of ice water! Immersing a heat stroke victim in ice water produces constriction of the blood vessels on the skin, which limits his ability to dissipate heat and causes him to shiver. Shivering is counterproductive since it generates even more heat. Ice packs placed against small areas of the skin, where large blood vessels course near the surface, maximize heat loss without causing vasoconstriction or shivering.

CHAPTER 26

Lightning and Electrical Injuries

LIGHTNING KILLS MORE PEOPLE EVERY year in the United States than all other natural disasters combined. Carrying or wearing metal objects—such as an ice ax, umbrella, backpack frame, or even a hairpin—increases the chances of being hit.

Other than cardiac arrest, the most devastating effects that can accompany an electrical injury are burns. Electrical burns account for about 6 percent of all admissions to burn units in the United States and for approximately eight hundred fatalities a year.

PREVENTION OF LIGHTNING INJURIES

There are a number of things that can be done to lessen your chances of being struck by lightning.

- When a thunderstorm threatens, seek shelter in a building or inside a vehicle.
- Avoid standing in small, isolated sheds or other small structures in open areas.
- In a forest, seek shelter in a low area under a thick growth of saplings or small trees.
- In an open area, go to a low place such as a ravine or valley.
- If you are totally in the open, stay far away from single trees to avoid lightning splashes. Drop to your knees and bend forward, putting your hands on your knees. Place insulating material (sleeping pad, life jacket, rope) between yourself and the ground. Do not lie flat on the ground.
- Do not stand underneath a tall tree in an open area or on a hilltop.
- If you are in a tent, stay as far away from the poles as possible.
- Get out of and away from open water.
- Get off motorcycles, bicycles, and golf carts. Put down golf clubs.
- Stay away from wire fences, clotheslines, metal pipes, and other metallic paths that could carry lightning to you from some distance.

☀ Lightning Injuries

Lightning can cause injuries in four ways:

1. *Direct hit.* In a direct hit, lightning directly strikes a person in the open who has been unable to find shelter. Lightning usually does not enter the body but instead is conducted over the skin surface ("flashover"), producing a variety of different injuries. The greatest damage may occur to skin beneath metal objects worn by the victim—such as jewelry, belt buckles, or zippers—which tend to increase the chance that the current will penetrate the body. Current may also penetrate the body through the eyes, ears, and mouth, causing deeper injuries to those parts. The victim is exposed to a tremendous electromagnetic field, which can disrupt the workings of the brain, lungs and heart and lead to a cardiac and respiratory arrest. Finally, the sudden vaporization of any moisture on the victim's skin can blast apart his clothing and shoes.

2. *Splash.* A more common scenario is for the victim to be struck by a lightning "splash," or "side flash," which occurs when a bolt first hits an object—such as a tree or another person—and then "jumps" to the victim.

3. *Step voltage.* In step-voltage injuries, lightning hits the ground or a nearby object, and the current spreads to the victims like a wave in a pond. Step voltage is often to blame when several people are hurt by a single lightning bolt.

4. *Blunt trauma.* The explosive force of the positive and negative pressure waves created by lightning, which are heard as thunder, can themselves cause blunt trauma, such as injuries to the spleen or liver or ruptured eardrums.

SIGNS AND SYMPTOMS

• *Heart and lungs:* Lightning disrupts the natural rhythm of the heart and paralyzes the lungs. About 75 percent of direct-strike victims and 55 percent of all victims suffer cardiopulmonary arrest (they have no pulse and are not breathing). The heart will often restart on its own, but because the lungs are still not working, the heart will stop again from lack of oxygen.

• *Brain and nervous system:* The victim may be knocked unconscious and suffer temporary paralysis, especially in the legs. Seizures, confusion, blindness, deafness, and inability to remember what happened may result.

• *Traumatic injuries:* Bruises, fractures, dislocations, spinal injury, and chest and abdominal injuries from the shock wave may occur. Ruptured eardrums can result in hearing loss.

• *Burns:* First- or second-degree burns are more common than severe burns after a lightning strike and form a distinctive featherlike or fern pattern on the skin (fig. 64).

TREATMENT

Note that lightning strike victims are not "charged" and thus pose no hazard to rescuers.

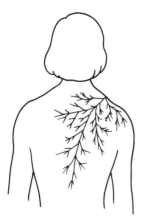

Figure 64. Fern pattern seen with lightning-strike burns.

1. If a victim is not breathing or has no pulse, start mouth-to-mouth rescue breathing (see p. 22) and cardiopulmonary resuscitation (CPR) (see p. 26).
2. Treatment of multiple lightning-strike victims differs from other situations in which there are several trauma victims. Rather than adhering to the standard rescue dogma of "ignore the victims who appear dead, and give priority to those who are still alive," with lightning-strike victims, give priority to the ones who appear dead since they may ultimately recover if properly resuscitated. The victims who are still breathing can usually wait.
3. Prolonged CPR may bring a lightning victim back to life since he is often just "shorted out" and not irreparably damaged. If you're successful in obtaining a pulse with cardiopulmonary resuscitation, continue rescue breathing until the victim begins to breathe on his own or you are no longer able to continue the resuscitation.
4. Stabilize and splint any fractures (see p. 77).
5. Initiate and maintain spinal precautions if indicated (see pp. 28–29).
6. Evacuate the victim to a medical facility as soon as possible (see Appendix C).

Electric Shock Injuries

Electricity will flow to the ground along the path of least resistance. Since cars are insulated from the ground by their rubber tires, a downed power line in contact with a car may leave the occupants unharmed as long as they remain inside the vehicle. If they step out of the car while holding onto the door, they may become a part of the grounding circuit and suffer electrical injury.

SIGNS AND SYMPTOMS

- When electricity traverses the body, it is converted to heat that burns the tissues in its path. The most severe burns occur under the skin to the muscles, nerves, and blood vessels, where you can't see them. Burns on the surface of the skin are not common.

- Cardiac arrest and death can result from the passage of current through the heart, lungs, or brain.
- Household current can produce intense muscle contractions, making it impossible for the victim to release the electrical object.

TREATMENT

1. Break the victim's contact with the electrical source as quickly and safely as possible. In a building, disconnect the plug of the offending appliance, or turn off the power at the fuse box. When the source of the current is a power line, call the fire department and electrical company. It is dangerous to touch a victim of electrical shock when he is still connected to the live source.
2. Once contact is broken, assess the victim for breathing and a pulse (see p. 16). If necessary begin CPR (see p. 26).
3. Evacuate the victim to a medical facility as soon as possible (see Appendix C). Be prepared to treat for shock (see p. 33) stemming from burns en route.

CHAPTER 27

Drowning

DROWNING IS THE SECOND MOST COMMON cause of accidental deaths among children and the third leading cause of death in young adults. A near-drowning is a submersion incident in which the victim survives for at least 24 hours after the event.

SIGNS AND SYMPTOMS

Signs and symptoms depend on how long the victim was under water. If less than one minute, the victim will probably be coughing, gagging, and choking, but will still be conscious and alert. As the submersion time exceeds more than one minute, there is progression to unconsciousness, and then respiratory and cardiac arrest.

TREATMENT

1. If a drowning victim is not breathing, mouth-to-mouth resuscitation (see p. 22) is the only first-aid treatment that matters. There is no value in attempting to clear the victim's lungs of water. The Heimlich maneuver (see p. 19) is not recommended unless you cannot obtain an airway because of an obstruction.

2. Expect the victim to vomit during rescue breathing. When he does, logroll him onto his side (see fig. 1) and sweep out the vomitus from his mouth. Then logroll him back over and continue the resuscitation.

3. Note any trauma, and take cervical spine precautions (see pp. 28–29) if indicated.

4. Check for a pulse (see fig. 12), and begin cardiopulmonary resuscitation (CPR) (see p. 26) if necessary.

5. All victims of a near-drowning should be taken to a hospital for evaluation, even if they appear fully recovered. Severe complications can develop even when the victim appears well during the first 6 to 12 hours after the event.

Following cold-water (less than 50 degrees Fahrenheit) submersion, several victims have been revived, even after 20 minutes of submersion (two have survived after more than 1 hour of submersion!). These remarkable saves are presumably due to the protective effects of profound hypothermia (see p. 166). If possible, perform CPR on cold-water drowning victims until they reach the hospital or until help arrives.

CHAPTER 28

Gastrointestinal (Abdominal) Problems

THE ABDOMEN, WITH ITS MANY ORGANS and intestines, can develop a variety of potentially serious problems. In the backcountry, the goal is to treat the symptoms and determine which problems require immediate evacuation.

Abdominal Pain ("Bellyaches")

Abdominal pain can be due to many causes, including constipation, gas, infection, inflammation, internal bleeding, ulcers, intestinal (bowel) obstruction, or aneurysms of major blood vessels. Abdominal pain can sometimes also be caused by pneumonia (see p. 210), a heart attack (see p. 202), kidney stones (see p. 73), pelvic problems, or diabetic ketoacidosis.

WHEN TO WORRY
Abdominal Pain

Any abdominal pain that lasts longer than 4 to 6 hours or is accompanied by frequent or projectile vomiting (vomit that seems to come out under pressure) or fever may indicate a serious illness. *If any of these symptoms are present, seek medical attention immediately.*

Some common causes of abdominal pain that require urgent medical evaluation are appendicitis, ulcer, bowel obstruction, urinary tract and pelvic infections, and any pain during pregnancy.

Appendicitis

The appendix is a small pouch about 3 or 4 inches long, located in the lower right side of the abdomen. Appendicitis occurs when the appendix becomes inflamed and swollen and fills with pus. Appendicitis can occur in persons of any age, but it is most common in young adults.

SIGNS AND SYMPTOMS

- The victim usually has a vague feeling of discomfort that often begins in the center of the upper abdomen and within a matter of hours moves to the lower right side.
- Pain is persistent and steady, but may be worsened by movement, sneezing, or coughing.
- There is usually loss of appetite, nausea, fever, and occasionally vomiting.
- Pressing on the stomach in the right lower quadrant (see fig. 21) produces an increased amount of pain.

TREATMENT

1. Do not give the victim anything to eat. If evacuation will take longer than 24 hours and the victim is not vomiting, administer small sips of water at regular intervals (every 15 minutes).
2. If available, administer a broad-spectrum antibiotic like cefalexin (Keflex®) 500 mg every 6 hours.
3. Avoid taking laxatives, which may worsen the problem.
4. Evacuate the victim to a medical facility as soon as possible (see Appendix C). Treatment almost always involves surgical removal of the appendix. Since the infected appendix may rupture and lead to peritonitis (a serious infection of the abdomen), the operation is usually performed as soon as possible.

Ulcer

An ulcer is an erosion or crater that develops in the lining of the stomach or small intestine.

SIGNS AND SYMPTOMS

- An ulcer usually produces persistent burning pain in the center of the upper abdomen, just below the solar plexus. The pain is occasionally relieved by eating and is often associated with nausea and belching. Sometimes an ulcer can be painless.
- Dark black stools may indicate that the ulcer is bleeding.

TREATMENT

1. Administer acid-reducing or acid-buffering medication such as Maalox®, Mylanta®, Tagamet®, Pepsid®, or Zantac®.
2. Avoid taking aspirin or nonsteroidal anti-inflammatory drugs such as ibuprofen (Motrin®).
3. Avoid alcohol, spicy foods, and tobacco.
4. Obtain medical evaluation as soon as possible.

Backcountry Tricks

Relieving Pain from Ulcers and Acid Indigestion

If you have pain from ulcers or acid indigestion, and are without any antacids, a glass of cold water alone will sometimes provide relief. A teaspoon or two of mentholated toothpaste, washed down with water or tea, will be even better. Avoid brands with baking soda or hydrogen peroxide.

Intestinal (Bowel) Obstruction

Bowel obstruction is a blockage of the intestines and occurs most commonly in individuals who have had previous abdominal surgery. It can also develop from infection or other causes like tumors or twisting of the bowel.

SIGNS AND SYMPTOMS

- Nausea, vomiting, and cramping abdominal pain.
- The victim's breath may have a fecal odor.
- The abdomen may look and feel distended.
- Pressing on the abdomen usually causes an increase in pain.

TREATMENT

1. Evacuate the victim to a medical facility as soon as possible (see Appendix C).
2. Do not give the victim anything to eat or drink, as it will produce vomiting.

Gallstones (Gallbladder Disease)

The gallbladder is connected to the underside of the liver and is located in the upper right part of the abdomen, just below the ribs (see fig. 21). Stones can form in the gallbladder and produce an obstruction.

SIGNS AND SYMPTOMS

- Pain and tenderness are present in the upper right side of the abdomen.
- Pushing under the rib cage on the right side of the abdomen while the victim takes a deep breath will increase the pain.
- The pain may radiate to the shoulder or back.
- Nausea and vomiting usually occur.

TREATMENT

1. Although gallstones are not immediately life threatening, it is best to evacuate the victim to a medical facility as soon as possible (see Appendix C).
2. Administer pain medication to the victim (see Appendix B).
3. Do not give the victim anything to eat. If evacuation will take longer than 24 hours and the victim is not vomiting, administer small sips of water at regular intervals (every 15 minutes).

Vomiting

Relatively benign causes of vomiting include motion sickness, emotional upset, food poisoning, viral illnesses (stomach flu or gastroenteritis), and pregnancy. Children can also vomit after deep coughing.

SIGNS AND SYMPTOMS

- Vomiting is the ejecting of partially digested food from the stomach through the mouth.

TREATMENT

1. Drink small but frequent amounts of a clear liquid such as soup, 7-Up®, or half-strength Gatorade®. The most frequent mistake made is drinking too much too soon; the stomach becomes distended, resulting in more vomiting.
2. Avoid solid food until the vomiting has stopped.

☀WHEN TO WORRY
Vomiting

Evacuate the victim to a medical facility as soon as possible if vomiting is associated with any of the following signs and symptoms:

- Head or abdominal trauma.
- Severe fatigue or confusion.
- Severe abdominal pain or abdominal distention.
- Vomit is bloody or has a coffee-grounds appearance.
- Fever greater than 101 degrees.
- Vomiting that continues for longer than 24 hours.

☼ Backcountry Tricks
Herbal Remedies for Nausea

Herbal remedies that may calm an upset stomach include ginger, peppermint, and chamomile. Ginger is especially useful for curbing the nausea caused by motion sickness. Ginger is ordinarily taken in the form of capsules, each containing 500 mg of the powdered herb. The average recommended daily dose is between 2 and 3 grams. It may also be consumed as a tea or in the extract form. There are no reports of severe toxicity in humans from eating recommended amounts of ginger.

WHEN TO WORRY
Diarrhea

Obtain medical assistance if diarrhea is accompanied by any of the following signs and symptoms:
- Blood or mucous in the stool.
- A fever greater than 101 degrees Fahrenheit.
- Severe abdominal pain or distention.
- Moderate to severe dehydration (see below).
- Diarrhea lasting longer than 3 days.

Diarrhea

Diarrhea is an increase in the frequency and looseness of stools. The most common cause of diarrhea in the United States is viral illness. Other causes include bacteria, parasites such as *Giardia* or *Cryptosporidium,* food allergies, inflammatory bowel disease, and anxiety.

Diarrhea that lasts only 1 to 2 days may not require any specific treatment. Frequent diarrhea (more than 10 stools a day) or diarrhea that lasts longer than 2 days may be serious and require specific treatment.

SIGNS AND SYMPTOMS
- More than three loose or watery stools per day.
- The stools may contain mucous, pus or blood, and be more foul smelling than normal.
- There may be abdominal cramps, malaise, nausea, vomiting, or fever.
- Severe or prolonged diarrhea can lead to dehydration. Dehydration can be mild, moderate, or severe.

Mild dehydration (3 to 5 percent weight loss)
- Thirsty; tacky mucous membranes (lips, mouth); normal pulse; dark urine.

Moderate dehydration (5 to 10 percent weight loss)
- Thirsty; dry mucous membranes; sunken eyes; small volume of dark urine; rapid and weak pulse.

Severe dehydration (greater than 10 percent weight loss)
- Drowsy or fatigued; very dry mucous membranes; sunken eyes; no urine; no tears; shock (rapid pulse or one that is thready or difficult to feel).

TREATMENT
1. *Replace fluids and electrolytes.* Oral rehydration with water and oral rehydration salts (ORS) (see below) is the most important treatment for

diarrhea illnesses in the backcountry. The fluids and electrolytes lost from infectious diarrhea are potentially fatal in children and can be devastating in adults. Diarrhea fluid contains sodium chloride (salt), potassium, and bicarbonate, so simply drinking plain water is inadequate replacement. Many glucose electrolyte solutions sold commercially are not ideal for replacement of diarrhea losses; the high concentration of sugar may increase fluid losses, and the electrolyte contents may not be optimal. Gatorade® can be used, but should be diluted to half-strength with water.

The World Health Organization recommends oral rehydration solutions containing the following combination of electrolytes added to 1 liter of water: sodium chloride, 3.5 g; potassium chloride, 1.5 g; glucose, 20 g; and sodium bicarbonate, 2.5 g. ORS packets can be purchased commercially (see Appendix A) or improvised.

Mild to moderately dehydrated adults should drink between 4 and 6 liters of oral rehydration solution in the first 4 to 6 hours. Children should be given 8 ounces of ORS every hour. Severe dehydration usually requires evacuation to a medical facility (see Appendix C) and intravenous fluids. Avoid using full-strength juices as a rehydration solution—juices often have three to five times the recommended concentration of sugar and can worsen the diarrhea.

2. *Administer antimotility drugs.* If the victim does not have bloody diarrhea or fever greater than 101 degrees Fahrenheit, loperamide (Imodium®) can be taken to reduce cramping and fluid losses associated with diarrhea. The dose for adults is 4 mg initially, followed by 2 mg after each loose bowel movement up to a maximum of 14 mg per day. Imodium® is preferred over Lomotil® because it has fewer potential side effects. Imodium® should not be given to children. Pepto-Bismol® and Kaopectate® are other commonly used antimotility drugs, but they are less effective.

3. *Administer antibiotics* (see Appendix B) if the diarrhea is accompanied by fever (101 degrees Fahrenheit or greater), if there is pus or blood in the stool, if the victim has signs and symptoms of giardiasis (see below), or if the victim is traveling in a Third World country with poor sanitation. Antibiotics that are effective include: ciprofloxacin (Cipro®), 500 mg twice a day for 3 days; trimethoprim/sulfamethoxazole (Septra® DS), 1 tablet twice a day for 3 days; or azithromycin (Zithromax®), 250 mg once a day for 3 days.

Backcountry Tricks

Improvising an Oral Rehydration Solution

You can improvise an oral rehydration solution from the following ingredients:
1 liter drinking water
1 teaspoon table salt
4 teaspoons cream of tartar (potassium bicarbonate)
½ teaspoon baking soda
4 tablespoons sugar

Another effective strategy is to alternate drinking two separate solutions prepared in the following manner:

Solution #1
8 ounces (250 ml) fruit juice
½ teaspoon honey or corn syrup
1 pinch salt

Solution #2
8 ounces (250 ml) water
¼ teaspoon baking soda

Giardiasis (Infection with Giardia lamblia)

It is almost impossible to visit a national park in the United States and not see a reminder that giardiasis has reached epidemic proportions. Giardia is the most common disease-causing intestinal parasite in the United States and one of the most common causes of diarrhea in Third World countries.

Giardia lamblia is a hearty parasite that can thrive even in very cold water. Just one glass of contaminated water in the backcountry is enough to produce illness.

SIGNS AND SYMPTOMS

- Symptoms are usually delayed for 7 to 10 days after drinking contaminated water and may last up to 2 months or longer if the infection is not treated.
- Onset is usually gradual, with 2 to 5 loose or mushy stools per day.
- Stools are mucousy and foul smelling.
- The victim usually experiences a rumbling or feeling in his gut, has foul-smelling gas, cramping abdominal pain, nausea, and burps that taste like rotten eggs.
- Weight loss can occur.

TREATMENT

1. Treat as for diarrhea (see above).
2. In the United States, giardiasis is usually treated with the prescription medication metronidazole (Flagyl®). The adult dose is 250 mg three times a day for 7 days. In Asia and South America, tinidazole (Tiniba®) is often used and can be taken as a single 2-gram dose to cure the infection.

Cryptosporidiosis (Crypto)

Cryptosporidium is a microscopic parasite that lives in the feces of infected humans and animals. When ingested by humans via contaminated water it produces diarrhea and abdominal cramping. It is found in nearly all surface waters that have been tested nationwide. In 1995, more than 45 million Americans drank water from sources that contained Crypto, and in Milwaukee in 1993, it produced the largest outbreak of waterborne diarrhea in United States history.

Cryptosporidium is a resilient parasite. It is not killed by chlorine or iodine at concentrations normally used to disinfect drinking water, and it can slip through many water filters. Since the parasite is between 2 and 5 microns in size, filters must be able to remove particles smaller than 2 microns to be effective against *Cryptosporidium*. Fortunately, the bug is very susceptible to heat and can be killed just by bringing water to a full boil.

SIGNS AND SYMPTOMS

- Symptoms usually begin 2 to 7 days after drinking contaminated water and can last for up to 2 to 3 weeks before resolving on their own.
- In most healthy people, *Cryptosporidium* causes abdominal cramps, low-grade fever, nausea, vomiting, and diarrhea, which can result in dehydration.
- For people with HIV/AIDS, on chemotherapy, or a weakened immune system, Crypto may last for months and can be fatal.

TREATMENT

1. Treat as for diarrhea (see above).
2. At this time, there is no reliable antibiotic treatment for Crypto. Some antibiotics that are presently being tested, and which may prove to be helpful, include paromycin, azithromycin (Zithromax®), itraconazole, and metronidazole (Flagyl®). Loperamide (Imodium®) may help decrease fluid losses and intestinal cramping (for dosage, see p. 192).

Traveler's Diarrhea

"Travelers' diarrhea" is usually caused by bacteria and afflicts almost 50 percent of visitors to developing countries that have poor sanitation and hygiene. Traveler's diarrhea is acquired through ingestion of contaminated food or water. Watching what you eat and drink may help but does not guarantee that you will not get sick.

When traveling, avoid drinking untreated tapwater or drinks with ice cubes. Bottled and carbonated drinks are generally safe. Avoid custards, salads, salsas, reheated food, milk, and unpeeled fruits and vegetables. Disinfect tapwater used for brushing teeth.

SIGNS AND SYMPTOMS

- Symptoms usually begin rather abruptly 2 to 3 days after arrival. The victim usually goes from feeling quite well to quite ill in a short period of time—an hour or so.
- The stools may contain mucous, pus, or blood, and be more foul smelling than normal.
- There may be abdominal cramps, malaise, nausea, vomiting, or fever.
- Severe or prolonged diarrhea can lead to dehydration. Dehydration can be mild, moderate, or severe (see above).

TREATMENT

1. Treat as you would for diarrhea (see above).
2. Antibiotics are very effective for treating most cases of traveler's diarrhea. The best antibiotics are ciprofloxacin (Cipro®), 500 mg twice a day for 2 to 3 days, and azithromycin (Zithromax®), 250 mg once a day for 2 to 3 days. It is well worth a visit to your physician for a prescription before your trip.
3. Bismuth subsalicylate (Pepto-Bismol®) is effective in preventing diarrhea in about 60 percent of travelers but must be taken in large quantities of 4 table-spoons four times a day, or 2 tablets four times a day.

Constipation

Constipation is delayed or difficult bowel movements with hard stools. It is a common problem when traveling in the wilderness because of disruption of normal habits. Constipation is easier to prevent than to treat. Drinking fluids to stay well hydrated and adjusting the diet to include fruit, vegetables, and whole grains is helpful.

SIGNS AND SYMPTOMS

- Delayed or difficult bowel movements.
- Hard stools.
- Abdominal pain.
- Bloating or abdominal distension.
- Vomiting may occur.

TREATMENT

1. A stool softener such as mineral oil or Metamucil® should be taken, with or without a gentle laxative such as prune juice or milk of magnesia.
2. If no stool has been passed for 5 to 10 days because of constipation, the stool may have to be removed from the rectum by using a gloved finger or an enema. This should be done carefully to prevent further injury to the anus and walls of the rectum.

CHAPTER 29

Genitourinary Problems

THE GENITOURINARY PARTS OF THE BODY include the "water works" organs—the kidneys, bladder and urethra—and the reproductive organs—the ovaries, uterus, fallopian tubes, vagina, and penis. Infections of the genitourinary parts are not uncommon while backpacking and can sometimes be easily treated without having to cut your trip short or see a physician. Occasionally problems in the genitourinary tract, such as an ectopic pregnancy, result in a life-threatening illness.

The urinary tract is divided into upper and lower regions. The upper urinary tract consists of the kidneys and two tubes (ureters) that carry urine to the bladder. The lower urinary tract consists of the bladder that holds the urine, and the urethra, the tube which drains the bladder to the outside world.

PREVENTION
- Drink plenty of fluids to maintain a clear-looking urine.
- After going to the bathroom, women should wipe themselves from front to back to avoid contaminating the urethral entrance with bacteria from the bowels.
- Don't postpone urinating when you feel the urge to go.
- Urinate immediately after sexual intercourse. This helps flush out any bacteria that may have accidentally been pushed into the urethra.
- In hot or humid conditions, wear loose-fitting pants and wipe the perineal area frequently with moist towelettes.
- Drinking cranberry juice may help prevent bladder infections by preventing bacteria from adhering to bladder cells. Unfortunately, other fruit juices have not been found to share this medicinal quality.

Urethral Infection (Urethritis)

Possible causes of urethral infection include sexually transmitted diseases, bacterial contamination from the rectum or vagina, trauma, and irritation from soap, spermicide, or other chemicals.

SIGNS AND SYMPTOMS

- The victim experiences burning pain upon urination and has the urge to urinate frequently.
- There may be a white or yellowish discharge from the tip of the urethra (sometimes it is also visible on the underwear).

TREATMENT

1. Infections of the urethra need to be treated with oral antibiotics such as azithromycin (Zithromax®)2 grams all at once or ciprofloxacin (Cipro®) 500 mg *plus* azithromycin 1 gram all at once.
2. Avoid washing or rinsing the genital area with potentially irritating soaps and chemicals.

Bladder Infection (Cystitis)

If you have to pull off the trail frequently to urinate, and it's painful, then you most likely have cystitis, a bladder infection. Although cystitis is not usually a serious disease, it is very uncomfortable, and if untreated, it can spread to the kidneys and produce a potentially dangerous condition.

Women are much more likely to develop a urinary tract infection than men, because the female urethra is much shorter and thus allows infection-causing bacteria a shorter, easier trip to the bladder, where they can multiply and produce an infection.

SIGNS AND SYMPTOMS

- The victim experiences burning pain upon urination and has the urge to urinate frequently.
- The urine can be cloudy, contain blood, and smell bad.
- There is often a dull pain or full sensation in the middle of the lower abdomen.

TREATMENT

1. Bladder infections are usually treated with a 3-day course of antibiotics such as trimethoprim/sulfamethoxazole (Septra DS®, Bactrim DS®) one pill twice a day or ciprofloxacin (Cipro®) 500 mg twice a day. Another prescription drug, phenazopyridine hydrochloride (Pyridium®), 200 mg every 4 to

6 hours, will help relieve pain and bladder spasms. It also turns urine and other body fluids reddish-orange, so don't wear contact lenses or expensive underclothes while taking it.

2. Drink lots of fluids, especially cranberry juice if available.

💣 WHEN TO WORRY
Kidney Infection (Pyelonephritis)

Kidney infections are potentially serious and can become life threatening if left untreated. Fortunately, most kidney infections can be easily treated with antibiotics.

SIGNS AND SYMPTOMS
- The victim often has the same symptoms as cystitis (see above) but in addition will often experience back pain (usually below the ribs in the flanks), chills, and fever.
- Nausea, vomiting, and abdominal pain may also be present.

TREATMENT
1. Individuals with a kidney infection need to be evacuated to a hospital as soon as possible (see Appendix C).
2. In transit, administer the same antibiotics that you would use for a bladder infection (see above) and continue antibiotic therapy for 10 days.

Kidney Stones

For signs, symptoms, and treatments, see p. 73.

💣 WHEN TO WORRY
Ectopic Pregnancy

Any abdominal or pelvic pain that is accompanied by vaginal bleeding and is not typical of a normal menstrual period should be evaluated by a physician immediately. An ectopic pregnancy (abnormal pregnancy in the fallopian tube) should be suspected if a menstrual period has been missed and vaginal bleeding and/or pelvic cramping occurs. The condition can rapidly become life threatening if not surgically treated.

Pelvic Infections (Pelvic Inflammatory Disease)

Pelvic Inflammatory Disease (PID) is the most common serious infection among reproductive-age women in the United States. It is usually casued by the same bacteria *(Gonorrhea and Chlamydia)* that are the infectious culprits in other sexually transmitted diseases.

SIGNS AND SYMPTOMS

- The victim experiences pelvic pain, usually associated with fever, chills, nausea, vomiting, and weakness.
- There is usually a yellow-green discharge from the vagina.

TREATMENT

1. Begin treatment with antibiotics (ciprofloxacin [Cipro®] 500 mg twice a day *plus* metronidazole [Flagyl®] 500 mg twice a day) as soon as possible. Continue antibiotic therapy for 2 weeks.
2. Evacuate the victim to a medical facility as soon as possible (see Appendix C).

Vaginal Yeast Infection (Candida Infection)

The most common cause of vaginal infections (vaginitis) is *Candida albicans,* a yeast-like organism. Wearing restrictive clothing and sweating for prolonged periods increase the likelihood of yeast infections. Other predisposing factors include the use of antibiotics, steroids, or oral contraceptives, pregnancy, or diabetes.

SIGNS AND SYMPTOMS

- Itching and irritation around the vaginal area.
- There is usually a white, creamy (cottage-cheese-like) discharge from the vagina. (A frothy, whitish gray vaginal discharge accompanied by abdominal pain and fever often indicates a bacterial infection requiring treatment with antibiotics.)

TREATMENT

Treat with antifungal medications such as clotrimazole (Gyne-Lotrimin®) vaginal tablets (7 days) or cream (14 days), or miconazole vaginal suppositories or cream.

An excellent alternative is fluconazole (Diflucan®); a single 150 mg tablet will cure most cases.

 Backcountry Tricks

Washing the Fungus Away

If antifungal medication is unavailable, a vinegar douche can be helpful in coping with vaginal yeast infections. Airing the vaginal area and switching to cotton underwear, or none at all, are also helpful.

CHAPTER 30

Allergic Reactions

ALLERGIC REACTIONS CAN OCCUR AS A result of insect stings (see Chapter 18), food allergies, medications, exposure to animals, and for other unknown reasons. The most severe form of an allergic reaction is anaphylactic shock, which can be life threatening within minutes after contact with the substance to which the individual is allergic.

☀WHEN TO WORRY
Severe Allergic Reactions (Anaphylactic Shock)

Anaphylactic shock from bee, wasp, hornet, and yellow-jacket stings is a common outdoor emergency. It is estimated that between 1 percent and 4 percent of the U.S. population is allergic to insect venom, and 40 to 50 deaths are reported annually.

SIGNS AND SYMPTOMS

- The victim may develop hives (red, raised skin welts), wheezing, tightness in the chest, shortness of breath, and a drop in blood pressure leading to dizziness, lightheadedness and fainting.
- The soft tissues of the throat, larynx, or trachea may swell, making it difficult or impossible for the person to swallow or breathe.

TREATMENT

1. The treatment for anaphylactic shock is epinephrine (adrenaline), and it needs to be given in the field. Epinephrine requires a prescription from your doctor. **People with bee sting or other serious allergies should carry injectable epinephrine with them at all times. There is no way to improvise epinephrine.**

2. Epinephrine is available in a spring-loaded injectable cartridge called the Epi E•Z Pen® that permits self-administration of the medicine without having

to deal with a needle and syringe. The device contains 2 ml of epinephrine 1:1000 USP in a disposable pushbutton spring-activated cartridge with a concealed needle. It will deliver a single dose of 0.3 mg epinephrine intramuscularly. For children who weigh less than 66 pounds, there is the Epi E•Z Pen® Jr. which contains one-half the dose of the adult injection. Instructions for use accompany the kits.

3. The Ana-Kit®, which contains a 1 ml pre-loaded syringe of epinephrine, can be substituted for the Epi E•Z Pen®. Although not as "user friendly" as the Epi E•Z Pen®, the Ana-Kit® syringe is more versatile because it can deliver two separate doses of 0.3 ml of epinephrine. Others in the party should also know how to use the Epi E•Z Pen® or Ana-Kit® in case the victim cannot help himself.

4. After administering epinephrine, give the victim oral diphenhydramine (Benadryl®), 25 to 50 mg every 4 to 6 hours. Diphenhydramine is an antihistamine and may lessen the allergic reaction.

5. After treatment, transport the victim to a medical facility immediately, as an anaphylactic reaction can recur once the epinephrine wears off.

Mild Allergic Reactions

All allergic reactions are not life threatening. Often one may develop only minor symptoms without wheezing or other breathing problems, chest tightness, or a drop in blood pressure.

SIGNS AND SYMPTOMS

- Hives (red, raised skin welts) and itching may be the only symptoms. The skin may become cherry red.
- Sneezing.
- Stuffy or runny nose.
- Watery, red eyes.
- Itching on the roof of the mouth.

TREATMENT

Mild allergic reactions may be managed with only an antihistamine, such as diphenhydramine (Benadryl®). For adults, 25 to 50 mg should be taken every 4 to 6 hours. The major side effect of this medication is drowsiness (see Appendix B).

CHAPTER 31

Heart Attack, Stroke, Seizures, and Diabetic Emergencies

AMONG THE UNEXPECTED MEDICAL emergencies that can arise in the backcountry are heart attacks, strokes, and seizures. Heart attacks and strokes kill more people in the United States each year than any other cause. Over 50 percent of these deaths occur before the individual reaches the hospital, thus it is very important to be able to recognize the signs and symptoms in order not to delay evacuation.

Heart Attack

A heart attack occurs when the blood supply to the heart muscle is reduced or completely blocked because of an obstruction in one of the arteries that supply blood to the heart. If blood flow is not restored within 1 to 6 hours, part of the heart muscle will die.

SIGNS AND SYMPTOMS

- The primary symptom of a heart attack is chest pain. The pain is usually a crushing or squeezing sensation located in the center of the chest; it may also radiate up into the neck and jaw or shoulders, or down the arms. The victim may also experience a tightness or crushing sensation across his chest. Sometimes there is only mild chest pain, or a burning sensation in the lower chest or upper abdomen near the solar plexus, or a feeling of indigestion.
- Cold sweats, nausea, vomiting, anxiety, shortness of breath, and weakness are often present.

TREATMENT

1. Aspirin may help to partially open the blocked artery. Have the victim either chew or swallow one aspirin tablet (325 mg).
2. If the victim has nitroglycerin tablets or spray, let him take them as prescribed.
3. If available, administer oxygen and pain medication (see Appendix B).
4. Keep the victim in a comfortable position.

5. Arrange immediate evacuation to a medical facility (see Appendix C) with the victim doing as little of the work as possible.

☄ Stroke

A stroke is a life-threatening event in which an artery to the brain bursts or becomes clogged by a blood clot, cutting off the supply of oxygen to a part of the brain. A stroke can affect the senses, speech, behavior, thought patterns, and memory. It may also result in paralysis, coma, and death.

SIGNS AND SYMPTOMS

Any or all of the following symptoms may be present:

- Sudden weakness or numbness of the face, arm, and leg, usually on one side of the body. One side of the victim's mouth may appear to droop.
- Loss of speech, or trouble talking or understanding speech.
- Loss of vision in only one eye.
- Sudden dizziness or loss of coordination.
- Sudden onset of a severe headache ("the worst headache of my life").

TREATMENT

1. The victim should be transported immediately to a medical facility (see Appendix C).
2. Continually reassess the victim's airway and level of consciousness (see p. 16), as his condition can worsen dramatically during transport.

☄ Seizures

Seizures can result from drugs, head injury, heat illness, low blood sugar (see p. 204), epilepsy, fever (in children), and other causes.

SIGNS AND SYMPTOMS

- With a grand mal (full body) seizure there is sudden loss of consciousness with the victim falling to the ground.
- The victim's body will stiffen and he will go into convulsions, jerking all parts of the body.
- Breathing will be labored and there may be frothing at the mouth.
- Normally, a seizure lasts 2 to 3 minutes. When the seizure ends, the victim's body relaxes, and he will be sleepy and confused for about 15 to 30 minutes.

TREATMENT

1. Do not try to restrain convulsive movements.
2. Move harmful objects out of the way.
3. Make sure the victim's airway is clear (see p. 16) and that he is breathing. If he is not breathing, start mouth-to-mouth rescue breathing (see p. 22).
4. Roll the victim onto his side to protect the airway if vomiting occurs.
5. Do not put anything in the victim's mouth.

6. Assist the victim to professional medical attention as soon as possible (see Appendix C).

DIABETIC EMERGENCIES

If a diabetic becomes confused, weak, or unconscious for no apparent reason, he may be suffering from insulin shock (low blood sugar) or diabetic ketoacidosis (high blood sugar).

Insulin Shock (Low Blood Sugar)

If a diabetic takes too much insulin or fails to eat enough food to match his insulin level or his level of exercise, a rapid drop in blood sugar can occur.

SIGNS AND SYMPTOMS
- Symptoms may come on very rapidly.
- The victim exhibits an altered level of consciousness, ranging from slurred speech, bizarre behavior, and loss of coordination, to seizures and unconsciousness.

TREATMENT
1. If still conscious, the victim should be given something containing sugar to drink or eat as rapidly as possible. This can be fruit juice, candy, or a nondiet soft drink.
2. Evacuate the victim to a medical facility as soon as possible (see Appendix C).

⚲ Backcountry Tricks
Treating Insulin Shock in an Unconscious Victim

If the victim is unconscious, place sugar granules, cake icing, or Glutose® paste from your first-aid kit under his tongue, where it will be rapidly absorbed.

Diabetic Ketoacidosis (High Blood Sugar)

Diabetic ketoacidosis (formerly called diabetic coma) comes on gradually as the result of insufficient insulin, which eventually leads to a buildup of a very high sugar (glucose) level in the victim's blood. Since the body cannot process the sugar due to lack of insulin, it breaks down the body's fat, producing an acidotic state (ketoacidosis).

SIGNS AND SYMPTOMS
- Early symptoms include frequent urination and thirst.
- Later, the victim will become dehydrated and confused or comatose, and will

develop nausea, vomiting, abdominal pain, and a rapid breathing rate, with a fruity odor to his breath.

TREATMENT

1. The victim needs immediate evacuation to a medical facility (see Appendix C).
2. If vomiting is not present and the victim is awake and alert, have him drink small, frequent sips of plain water.
3. If you are unsure whether the victim is suffering from insulin shock (low blood sugar) (see above) or ketoacidosis (high blood sugar), it is always safer to assume it is low blood sugar and administer sugar.

CHAPTER 32

Respiratory Infections

RESPIRATORY INFECTIONS ARE VERY COMMON and encompass all of the cold and flu syndromes, sore throats, sinus infections, ear infections, and illnesses that make you cough, including bronchitis and pneumonia.

Colds and Flu

Both colds and flu are caused by viruses that are present in the environment and are spread from person to person in droplets expelled during sneezing, coughing, speaking, or intimate contact. The average person has fifty or more colds in a lifetime. Contrary to popular belief, a cold is not brought on by being cold, by having wet feet or clothes, or by going outdoors with wet hair. However, being overly tired or stressed can depress your immune system and make you more vulnerable to developing either a cold or a flu.

SIGNS AND SYMPTOMS

- The most common symptoms of a cold are a runny nose, sore throat, hoarseness, congestion, and cough. Some colds may produce all of these symptoms, or a cold sufferer may have only one or two.
- Flu sufferers are more likely to have a headache, especially behind the eyes, muscle aches and pains, and high fevers.

TREATMENT

1. There is no "antibiotic" available yet for colds. Antibiotics fight bacterial infections, and unfortunately colds and flu's are viral infections.
2. Most colds and flu's run their course in 5 to 10 days regardless of what a person does.
3. Nonprescription cold medications containing decongestants, antihistamines, and expectorants can help ease the symptoms and allow the victim to better tolerate the cold until his own immune system fights off the infection.
4. Gargling with a warm saltwater solution may relieve a sore throat. Much of the conventional folklore about treating a cold—such as feeding a fever, starving

a cold, or taking laxatives—has no real basis in fact. There is also no solid evidence that taking large doses of vitamin C has any effect on a cold.

5. Echinacea and goldenseal—a combination herbal remedy that has been shown to boost the immune system—may be beneficial.

Bacterial Sore Throats (Strep Throat)

Sore throats caused by bacteria can be difficult to differentiate from sore throats caused by a virus.

SIGNS AND SYMPTOMS

- High fevers (over 102 degrees Fahrenheit).
- Exudate or pus on the victim's tonsils (back of the throat).
- Muffled voice.
- Lumps (enlarged lymph nodes) in the neck.

TREATMENT

Bacterial sore throats require treatment with antibiotics such as penicillin or erythromycin (see Appendix B).

💣 WHEN TO WORRY
Severe Strep Throat

If the victim cannot swallow his secretions or open his mouth fully, he should be evacuated immediately to a medical facility for treatment. Antibiotics, if available, should be administered en route (see Appendix C).

💣 Sinus Infection (Sinusitis)

Bacterial infection of the sinuses usually accompanies or follows a cold or hay fever.

SIGNS AND SYMPTOMS

- The most prominent symptom of a sinus infection is a headache or sense of heaviness above the eyes or alongside the nose.
- Drainage into the nose or back of the throat, nasal congestion, low-grade fevers, and tenderness while pressing over the infected sinus may also be present.
- Pain may also be referred to the upper jaw or teeth.

TREATMENT

1. Treatment consists of antibiotics (see Appendix B), decongestants, and antihistamines.

2. The victim should seek medical care as soon as possible. Emergency evacuation is not usually necessary unless the symptoms are progressing rapidly or the victim develops swelling around the eyes or nose.

Middle Ear Infection (Otitis Media)

Middle ear infections usually precede or accompany a cold, sore throat, or sinus infection.

SIGNS AND SYMPTOMS

- The predominant symptom is throbbing or stabbing pain in the ear.
- The victim may experience decreased or muffled hearing, fever, and nausea.
- Occasionally, a purulent (pus-filled) discharge may exude from the ear.

TREATMENT

1. Administer an antibiotic such as amoxicillin (Amoxil®) or trimethoprim/ sulfamethoxazole (Septra® DS) for 10 days (see Appendix B).
2. Administer a decongestant such as pseudoephedrine hydrochloride (Sudafed®) 60 mg every 4 to 6 hours.

Outer Ear Infection ("Swimmer's Ear")

Swimmer's ear is a swelling and infection of the outer ear canal caused by repeated exposure of the ear canal to water and bacteria. The water macerates the lining of the outer ear canal, which provides a better habitat for bacteria to proliferate.

Prevention. After swimming, cleanse and dry the ear canal with drops containing equal parts of rubbing alcohol and white vinegar. Never use a cotton swab to clean the ear.

SIGNS AND SYMPTOMS

- Often the first sign of swimmer's ear is itching and slight irritation in the ear canal.
- Within a few hours to a day, the ear can become red and extremely painful and drain pus or yellowish fluid.
- Unlike individuals with middle ear infections, victims of outer ear infections will have severe pain when you pull on the ear lobe or push against their outer ear.

TREATMENT

1. Place 2 to 3 antibiotic ear drops containing polymyxin B and neomycin, or colistin sulfate with hydrocortisone (Cortisporin® Otic Suspension), into the outer ear canal four times a day for 4 to 5 days.
2. Keep all water out of the ear for 2 to 3 weeks.

Backcountry Tricks
Treating Swimmer's Ear

If you don't have antibiotic ear drops, one part household vinegar diluted with four parts fresh water or rubbing alcohol may be used as a substitute.

Bronchitis

Bronchitis is an infection of the air passages leading from the windpipe to the lungs. It is usually caused by the same viruses that are responsible for colds and other upper respiratory infections. Sometimes it can be due to a bacterial infection. Bronchitis often begins as a cold that "settles in the chest."

SIGNS AND SYMPTOMS

- Inflammation of the lining of the bronchial tubes leads to secretion of mucous that irritates the airway and results in coughing. The cough may be dry or produce thick yellow or greenish phlegm.
- Bronchitis also may produce a pain in the upper chest that worsens with coughing or deep breathing.
- Victims with bronchitis usually are not short of breath and do not have a rapid respiratory rate.
- Fever is not usually present.

TREATMENT

1. Cough expectorants, which help bring up phlegm, may be useful. Cough syrups containing cough suppressants, such as codeine, impair the body's normal process for expelling phlegm. Save them for nighttime use to help you sleep.
2. Drink plenty of fluids to help thin the mucous and make it easier to expel.
3. Breathing in warm, humidified air can also loosen secretions and aid expectoration.
4. Most cases of bronchitis resolve themselves in a week or so.
5. If cough produces yellow or greenish sputum, antibiotics such as erythromycin or azithromycin may be administered (see Appendix B).

☀WHEN TO WORRY
Severe Bronchitis

If self-care does not lead to improvement within 1 week, or if you develop shortness of breath, fever above 101 degrees Fahrenheit, wheezing, severe pain in the chest, or cough productive of blood-specked or greenish phlegm, you should see a physician as soon as possible.

●☀WHEN TO WORRY
Pneumonia

Pneumonia is an infection of the lungs. It can be caused by bacteria or viruses, or by physical or chemical agents.

SIGNS AND SYMPTOMS

• Pneumonia causes a cough which usually produces green or yellowish phlegm.
• Fever, shaking, chills, and weakness are present.
• Stabbing chest pain, often made worse with each breath, shortness of breath, and rapid breathing may also occur.
• Pneumonia can sometimes also cause abdominal pain, especially in children.

TREATMENT

1. Administer antibiotics such as azithromycin (Zithromax®), amoxicillin (Amoxil®), or erythromycin (see Appendix B).
2. The victim should seek professional medical care as soon as possible.

The Wilderness First-Aid Kit (Excluding Medications)

A first-aid kit is one of the wilderness "ten essentials"—the basic things that *everyone* should have on *every* backcountry trip. Like most backpackers, I am obsessed with finding imaginative ways to limit the size and weight of the equipment I carry on outings. True to this philosophy, for many years I carried only a long piece of transplanted duct tape wrapped around a water bottle and some Band-Aids® "in the event of an emergency." Although duct tape is certainly a "don't-leave-home-without-it" commodity, it has serious limitations as a one-item first-aid kit.

DESIGNING THE WILDERNESS FIRST-AID KIT

When designing a wilderness first-aid kit, you will need to consider several variables:

- Your medical expertise
- The location and environmental extremes of your destination
- Diseases that may be particular to an area of travel
- The duration of travel
- The distance you will be from definitive medical care and the availability of professional rescue
- The number of people the kit will need to support
- Preexisting illnesses in your party members
- Weight and space limitations

The wilderness medical kit should be well organized in a protective and convenient carrying case or pouch. For backpacking, trekking, or hiking, a nylon organizer bag is optimal. Bags with clear protective vinyl compartments have proven superior to mesh-covered pockets. The vinyl protects the components from dirt, moisture, and insects and prevents the items from falling out when the kit is turned on its side or upside down.

For aquatic or marine environments, the kit should be stored in a waterproof drybag or watertight hard container. Inside, items should be sealed in zip-locked bags since moisture will invariably make its way into any container.

Some medicines may need to be stored outside of the main kit to ensure protection from extreme temperatures. Capsules and suppositories melt when exposed to body-temperature (99-degree) heat, while many liquid medicines become useless after freezing.

THE BASIC WILDERNESS KIT
Equipment
Sam® Splint. A versatile and lightweight foam-padded aluminum splint, adaptable for use on almost any part of the body. Can be fashioned into a cervical collar, into an arm, leg, or ankle splint.

Hyperthermia/hypothermia thermometer. Ideally should be able to read body temperatures down to 85 degrees and up to 107 degrees Fahrenheit.

CPR Microshield mask. A compact and easy-to-use clear, flexible barrier with a one-way air valve for performing mouth-to-mouth rescue breathing. The shield prevents physical contact with the victim's secretions.

Bandage scissors. Designed with a blunt tip to protect the victim while you cut through clothes, boots, or bandages.

Cotton-tipped swabs (Q-tips®). Can be used to remove insects or other foreign material from the eye. Also useful to roll fluid out from beneath a blister, or to evert an eyelid to locate a foreign body.

Safety pins. Useful in improvising many items of first-aid equipment.

Duct tape. Useful in improvising sunglasses, splints, traction splints, and wound closure strips, and for general repair.

Accident report form

Pencil

Plastic resealable zip-locked bags. Useful in improvised techniques such as wound and eye irrigation and cervical spine stabilization.

Wound Management Items
10–20 cc irrigation syringe with an 18-gauge catheter tip. Can be used like a squirt gun to flush out germs from wounds without harming the delicate tissues.

Povidone-iodine solution USP 10 % (Betadine®). Use to disinfect backcountry water and to sterilize wound edges. When diluted 10-fold with water, can be used for wound irrigation.

¼ by 4 inch wound closure strips. Excellent for closing cuts in the wilderness. Stronger, longer, stickier, and more porous than butterfly-type adhesive bandages.

Tincture of benzoin. A liquid adhesive that enhances the stickiness of wound closure strips, moleskin, or tape.

Double antibiotic ointment (Polysporin®). A topical antibacterial ointment that helps prevent minor skin infections and accelerates wound healing. Avoid triple antibiotic ointments with neomycin—they can produce an allergic rash in susceptible individuals.

Forceps or tweezers. For removing embedded objects from the skin such as splinters, cactus thorns, ticks, or stingers.

First-aid cleansing pads with lidocaine. These pads have a textured surface that makes them ideal for scrubbing dirt and embedded objects out of "road rash" types of abrasions. Lidocaine is a topical anesthetic.

Antiseptic towelettes with benzalkonium chloride. Disposable wipes that may be used to clean wounds. Benzalkonium chloride may help to kill the rabies virus on wounds inflicted by animals.

Surgical scrub brush. A sterile scrub brush for cleaning embedded objects and dirt from abrasions.

Aloe vera gel. A topical anti-inflammatory gel for treating burns, frostbite, blisters, abrasions, poison oak, poison ivy, and poison sumac.

SuperGlue®. Useful in improvised techniques such as making wound closure strips and closing blisters.

Latex or nitrile gloves. To protect the rescuer from blood-borne infectious diseases such as hepatitis and AIDS. Latex may cause a life-threatening allergic reaction in susceptible individuals or a red and itchy rash on the skin. If you or the victim may be allergic to latex, use nitrile gloves.

Bandage Material

4 by 4 inch sterile dressings. For applying pressure to a wound to stop bleeding or to make a pressure dressing.

Nonadherent sterile dressings (Aquaphor®, Xeroform®, Adaptic®, Telfa®), or Spenco 2nd Skin®. Nonadherent sterile dressings are used to cover abrasions, burns, lacerations, and blisters. Spenco 2nd Skin® is an excellent alternative and provides an ideal covering for burns, blisters, abrasions, and cuts.

214 ▼ APPENDIX A

It is a polyethylene oxide gel laminate composed of 96 percent water that cools and soothes on contact and can be left in place for up to 48 hours.

Gauze roller bandages or Kling®. Sterile bandage used to keep dressings in place and further protect a wound from the environment.

Elastic roller bandage or Ace® wrap. Used to hold dressings in place or to create a pressure bandage for bleeding or sprains.

Assortment of strip and knuckle adhesive bandages

Stockinette bandage. A net-style bandage particularly useful for holding dressings in place across a joint.

Molefoam. A thick, padded adhesive material for protecting blisters. Cut a donut out of the material and place it around a blister site.

Moleskin. A thin, padded adhesive material for protecting skin from developing blisters.

Tape. Athletic tape 1" x 10 yards.

Basic Dental Kit
Dental floss
Dental wax
Cotton rolls
Cavit® temporary filling material
Zinc oxide
Eugenol (oil of cloves)

Miscellaneous
Glutose® paste. Oral glucose gel containing concentrated sugar for treating hypoglycemia and insulin reactions in diabetics, as well as hypothermia.

SPECIFIC SUPPLIES FOR EXTREME ENVIRONMENTS
High Risk of Venomous Snakes
Sawyer Extractor®. A vacuum pump device that provides 1 atmosphere of negative pressure for potentially removing the venom of poisonous snakebites. (Made by Sawyer Products, 1-800-940-4464; available in outdoor equipment stores.)

Elastic roller bandage or Ace® wrap. To apply the Australian compression and immobilization technique for isolating the snake venom after a snakebite.

High Risk of Altitude Illness
Oxygen
Portable hyperbaric bag (Gamow® Bag)

Acetazolamide (Diamox®)
Dexamethasone (Decadron®)
Nifedipine (Procardia®)

High Risk of Snow Blindness

Opthalmic anesthetic (proparacaine or tetracaine 0.5%). To facilitate eye examination and to provide short-term analgesia.

Fluorescein stain. For diagnosing corneal abrasions.

Opthalmic cycloplegic (cyclopentolate 1%). For relieving pain associated with snowblindness.

Opthalmic corticosteroid-antibiotic combination (Maxitrol®)

Opthalmic antibiotic eyedrops (Tobrex®)

Hot Climate

Hyperthermia thermometer

Intravenous normal saline solutions and administration supplies

Chemical ice packs

Oral rehydration salt packets (electrolyte salts and glucose). When combined with a liter of water, they provide an ideal solution for replacing electrolytes and fluids lost during diarrhea illness, heat exhaustion or vomiting. (Made by Adventure Medical Kits, 1-800-324-3517; available in outdoor equipment stores.)

Cold Climate

Hypothermia thermometer. Reads down to at least 85 degrees Fahrenheit.

Matches

Glutose® paste. Concentrated sugar to help the body generate heat.

Travel in Jungle or Developing Countries

Oral rehydration salt packets

Antibiotics: ciprofloxacin (Cipro®) or azithromycin (Zithromax®). For treating "traveler's diarrhea."

Loperamide (Imodium®). For symptomatic relief of diarrhea.

Clotrimazole (Lotrimin®) or betamethasone dipropionate cream (Lotrisone®). For treating fungal infections.

Permethrin 5% cream and 1% shampoo. For treating lice, bedbugs, and scabies.

Insect repellent

🔆 Backcountry Tricks
Improvised Uses for a Safety Pin

- To pin the tongue to the lower lip (using two safety pins) to establish an airway in an unconscious victim (see fig. 7).
- To replace a lost screw in eyeglasses to prevent the lens from falling out.
- To improvise eyeglasses: Draw two circles in a piece of duct tape where your eyes would fit. Use the pin to make holes in the circles and then tape this to your face. The pinholes will partially correct near-sighted vision.
- To check sensation on the skin as part of a neurologic exam.
- To punch a hole in a plastic bag filled with water for wound and eye irrigation.
- To remove an embedded foreign object from the skin (see p. 155).
- To pop an abscess or a blister.
- To burn a small hole (heat the safety pin with a match first) in the nail to drain a subungal hematoma—a blood clot under a traumatized nail, which produces exquisite pain.
- To make a fish hook.
- To make a finger splint.
- To make a sewing needle, using dental floss as thread.
- To hold gaping wounds together.
- To replace a broken zipper on clothing.
- To hold gloves or mittens to your coat sleeve.
- To unclog jets in camping stoves.
- To pin triage notes to multiple victims.
- To fashion a shoulder or arm immobilizer (see figs. 27 and 28).
- To fix a ski binding.
- To remove a thrombosed hemorrhoid.

Medications

NON-PRESCRIPTION (OVER-THE-COUNTER) MEDICATIONS

Warning: Consult your physician regarding any medication that you carry in your first-aid kit and inquire about any potential complications or side effects before you depart. A physician should always be consulted before any medication is taken by a child, infant, pregnant woman, or nursing mother. Read the instructions carefully on the medication package and do not use if you think you may be allergic to the drug. Sharing medications with others is potentially dangerous and is not generally recommended.

Pain, Fever, and Inflammation

Ibuprofen (Motrin®, Advil®)

Indications: For the temporary relief of minor aches and pains associated with the common cold, headache, toothache, muscular aches, backache, and arthritis. Also effective in reducing the inflammation associated with sprains, strains, bursitis, tendinitis, minor burns, and frostbite. Reduces the pain of menstrual cramps and lowers fever. Excellent for the treatment of kidney-stone pain.

Dosage: Adults: 400 to 800 mg every 8 hours with food. Do not take on an empty stomach. Children: Ibuprofen is available by prescription in a liquid form for children.

Warning: Do not take Ibuprofen if you are allergic to aspirin or any other nonsteroidal anti-inflammatory drug. It may cause upset stomach or heartburn. Do not use if you have gastritis, ulcers, or are prone to bleeding or on any blood thinner medication. Not recommended for use during pregnancy. Avoid if you have kidney problems.

Acetaminophen (Tylenol®)

Indications: For relief of pain and fever. Tylenol® has no anti-inflammatory effect.

Dosage: Adults: 1000 mg every 4 to 6 hours. Children: 15 mg/kg (to convert pounds to kg divide by 2.2) every 4 to 6 hours.

Warning: In case of overdose, contact a physician or poison control center immediately. Do not use this drug if you have any liver disease, or if you regularly consume alcohol. Avoid if you have an allergy to this medicine.

Allergic Reactions and Motion Sickness
Diphenhydramine (Benadryl®)

Indications: Diphenhydramine is an antihistamine that can temporarily relieve runny nose, sneezing, watery eyes, and itchy throat due to hay fever or other respiratory allergies and colds. Relieves itching and rash associated with allergic reactions, and poison oak or ivy. Useful as an adjunct to epinephrine in the treatment of severe allergic shock. May also prevent and help relieve the symptoms of motion sickness.

Dosage: Adults: 25 to 50 mg every 4 to 6 hours. Children: consult your physician.

Warning: May cause drowsiness. Individuals with asthma, glaucoma, high blood pressure, emphysema, or prostatic enlargement should not use unless directed by a physician. Not recommended for use in hot environments, when heat illness is likely, during pregnancy, or while taking other antihistamines.

Skin Rashes
Hydrocortisone cream USP 1%

Indications: For temporary relief of minor skin irritations and allergic reactions.

Dosage: Adults and children 2 years of age and older: apply to affected area not more than three to four times a day. Children under two: consult a physician.

Warning: If condition worsens or if symptoms persist for more than 7 days or clear up and occur again within a few days, stop use of this product and do not begin use of any other hydrocortisone product unless you have consulted a physician. Do not use for the treatment of diaper rash. For external use only. Avoid contact with eyes.

Antacids
Aluminum hydroxide and simethicone tablets (Mylanta®)

Indications: Each tablet contains both an antacid and an anti-gas ingredient. Helps relieve heartburn, acid indigestion, sour stomach, and gas. Provides symptomatic relief of peptic ulcer disease and gastritis.

Dosage: Two to four tablets between meals and at bedtime.

Warning: Do not use Mylanta® if you have kidney disease. It can interfere with the absorption of certain antibiotics. If symptoms persist, consult a physician as soon as possible.

Burns and Frostbite
Aloe Vera Gel
Indications: A topical (placed on the skin) treatment for first-degree and second-degree burns, frostbite, abrasions and blisters.

Dosage: Apply a thin coat to the affected area two to three times a day.

Warning: Discontinue use if redness, swelling, or pain develops at the site.

Wounds
Topical Antibiotic Ointment (Polysporin®)
Indications: A topical (placed on the skin) antibiotic that can be applied to wounds to help prevent infection and facilitate healing. Also helps to treat minor infections and burns.

Dosage: Apply a thin coat of ointment directly over the wound or cut (do not place inside the cut) at least three times a day.

Warning: Discontinue use if redness, swelling, or pain develops at the site.

Symptomatic Relief of Diarrhea
Loperamide (Imodium®) 2 mg capsules
Indications: For controlling the abdominal cramping and diarrhea associated with intestinal infections.

Dosage: 4 mg initially, followed by one capsule (2 mg) after each loose bowel movement not to exceed 14 mg in one day.

Warning: Imodium® should not be used if there is associated fever (temperature greater than 101 degrees F), blood or pus in the stool, or the abdomen becomes swollen. It should not be used for more than 48 hours. Do not give this drug to children.

Bismuth subsalicylate (Pepto-Bismol®)
Indications: May prevent and help treat traveler's diarrhea, relieve nausea, and upset stomach.

Dosage: Two tablets four times a day.

Warning: This medication should not be used by individuals allergic to aspirin. It should not be used to treat vomiting in children and teenagers who have or are recovering from chicken pox or flu. If vomiting occurs, consult a physician as this could be an early sign of Reyes Syndrome, a rare but serious illness. As with any drug, if you are pregnant or nursing a baby, seek the advice of a health professional before using.

PRESCRIPTION MEDICATIONS

Warning: Consult your physician regarding any medication that you carry in your first-aid kit and inquire about any potential complications or side effects before you depart. A physician should always be consulted before any medication is taken by a child, infant, pregnant woman, or nursing mother. Read the instructions carefully on the medication package and do not use if you think you may be allergic to the drug. Sharing medications with others is potentially dangerous and is not generally recommended. Doses listed are for adults only, unless otherwise noted.

Severe Allergic Reactions (Anaphylactic Shock)

Epi E•Z Pen® (Epinephrine auto-injector) and Epi E•Z Pen® Jr.

Epinephrine quickly constricts blood vessels, and relaxes smooth muscles. It improves breathing, stimulates the heart to beat faster and harder, and relieves hives and swelling.

Indications: Emergency treatment of severe allergic reactions (anaphylaxis) to bees, wasps, hornets, yellow jackets, foods, drugs, and other allergens. May also help relieve symptoms of asthma.

Dosage: For adults and children over 66 lbs: Each Epi E•Z Pen® contains 2 ml of epinephrine 1:1000 USP in a disposable push-button, spring-activated cartridge with a concealed needle. It will deliver a single dose of 0.3 mg epinephrine intramuscularly. Pull off the cap and place the black tip against the thigh. Press the gray button on top of the auto-injector down with your thumb to release a spring activated plunger, and push a concealed needle into the thigh muscle. The drug should be felt within 1 to 2 minutes.

For children who weigh less than 66 lbs: The Epi E•Z Pen® Jr. will deliver a single dose of 0.15 mg of epinephrine.

Warning: Epinephrine should be avoided in individuals who are older than 50 years of age, or who have a known heart condition unless the situation is life threatening. Sometimes a single dose of epinephrine may not be enough to completely reverse the effects of an anaphylactic reaction. For individuals who know they have severe allergic reactions, it may be wise to carry more than one auto-injector.

Oral Antibiotics

Some of the antibiotics listed below have similar uses and overlapping spectrums of antibacterial activity. Before departing on your trip, discuss with your physician which antibiotics best suit your needs.

Azithromycin (Zithromax®) 250 mg capsules

This is a broad-spectrum, erythromycin-type antibiotic. It is more potent than erythromycin, causes less side effects, and only has to be taken once a day for 5 days.

Indications: Tonsillitis, ear infections, bronchitis, pneumonia, sinusitis, traveler's diarrhea, skin infections, urethritis, pelvic infections.

Dosage: Take two capsules on the first day, followed by one capsule a day for 4 more days. For urethritis take 1 to 2 grams one time (see p. 197).

Warning: Do not use if you are allergic to erythromycin. Do not use simultaneously with the antihistamines Seldane® or Hismanal®.

Amoxicillin Clavulanate (Augmentin®) 500 mg tablets

A broad-spectrum penicillin-type antibiotic.

Indications: Bite wounds, skin infections, pneumonia, urinary tract infections, ear infections, bronchitis, tonsillitis and sinusitis.

Dosage: One tablet every 8 hours, for 7 to 10 days.

Warning: Do not use if allergic to penicillin. Stop use if rash develops. May cause diarrhea.

Ciprofloxacin (Cipro®) 500 mg tablets

Indications: Diarrhea including traveler's diarrhea, pneumonia, bronchitis, urinary tract infections (urethritis, cystitis, pyelonephritis), pelvic infections, bone infections.

Dosage: One tablet twice a day, for 3 days. For kidney infections, pelvic infections, pneumonia and bone infections, treat for 7 to 10 days.

Warning: Not recommended for patients less than 18 years old or pregnant or nursing women. Adverse effects, although uncommon, have included nausea, vomiting, diarrhea, and abdominal pain.

Erythromycin 250/500 mg tablets

An alternative antibiotic for individuals allergic to penicillin.

Indications: Bronchitis, tonsillitis, pneumonia, skin infections, sinus infections, strep throat, ear and eye infections.

Dosage: 250 to 500 mg every 6 hours, for 7 to 10 days.

Warning: May cause upset stomach, vomiting, and/or diarrhea. Take with food. Do not use simultaneously with the antihistimines Seldane® or Hismanal®.

Cefuroxime (Ceftin®) or Cephalexin (Keflex®) 250 to 500 mg tablets

Broad-spectrum antibiotics which can be substituted for Augmentin® in individuals allergic to penicillin.

Indications: Skin and wound infections, bronchitis, urinary tract infections, middle ear infections (otitis media), some bone infections, bite wounds, tonsillitis, dental infections, sinusitis.

Dosage: 250 to 500 mg every 6 hours.

Warning: Avoid, or use with caution, in individuals with penicillin allergy, since 5 percent of people may be cross-reactive.

Metronidazole (Flagyl®) 250 mg tablets

Indications: Infections with giardia or amoebae; intra-abdominal infections including peritonitis and appendicitis, dental infections, pelvic infections.

Dosage: Giardiasis: one tablet three times a day, for 7 days. Amoebiasis: three tablets three times a day, for 5 to 10 days. Other intra-abdominal or pelvic infections: two tablets every 6 hours if the patient is not vomiting.

Warning: Do not drink alcohol while taking this medication. The interaction will cause severe abdominal pain, nausea, and vomiting. May cause unpleasant metallic taste. Do not use during pregnancy.

Trimethoprim/Sulfamethoxazole (Septra DS®; Bactrim DS®)

Each tablet contains 80 mg trimethoprim and 400 mg sulfamethoxazole.

Indications: Urinary tract or kidney infections, middle ear (otitis media) and sinus infections, and bronchitis. Can be substituted for ciprofloxacin to treat traveler's diarrhea or dysentery. It is cheaper than ciprofloxacin, but some bacteria which cause dysentery have developed resistance to this drug.

Dosage: One tablet twice a day for 5 days for diarrhea and dysentery. Other infections may require a 10-day course.

Warning: Do not use in individuals allergic to sulfa drugs. Trimethoprim 200 mg alone twice a day, may be substituted for treatment of diarrhea and dysentery. Discontinue use at the first sign of skin rash or any adverse reaction. Do not use in pregnancy.

Penicillin (Pen Vee®K) 250 mg tablets

Indications: Strep throat, tonsillitis, and dental infections.

Dosage: One tablet every 6 hours for 7 to 10 days.

Warning: Do not use if allergic to penicillin. Stop use if rash develops. May cause diarrhea.

Amoxicillin (Amoxil®) 250 mg tablets

Indications: Middle ear infections (otitis media), sinus infections, tonsillitis, bronchitis.

Dosage: One tablet every 6 hours for 10 days.

Warning: Do not use if allergic to penicillin. Stop use if rash develops. May cause diarrhea.

Neomycin and polymyxin B sulfates and hydrocortisone otic suspension (Cortisporin® Otic Suspension)

Indications: External ear infections ("Swimmers Ear").

Dosage: Four drops instilled into the affected ear four times a day.

Warning: Discontinue using if a rash develops or the condition worsens.

Tobramycin (Tobrex®) Opthalmic Solution 0.3%

Indications: For external infections of the eye (conjunctivitis or pink eye, or corneal abrasions).

Dosage: One to two drops into the affected eye every 2 hours while awake.

Warning: Do not use if you develop or have an allergy or sensitivity to this medicine.

Nausea and Vomiting
Prochlorperazine (Compazine®) or Promethazine HCL (Phenergan®) 25 mg Suppositories

Indications: For control of severe nausea and vomiting.

Dosage: 25 mg rectally twice a day.

Warning: Do not use in children. Side effects include neck spasm, difficulty in swallowing and talking, sensation that the tongue is thick, muscle stiffness, and agitation. If these symptoms occur, discontinue use of the drug and administer Benadryl® 50 mg. May produce drowsiness.

Pain Medication
Hydrocodone 5 mg and Acetaminophen 500 mg (Vicodin®)

Indications: For relief of pain. Can also be used for relief of diarrhea and suppression of coughs.

Dosage: One to two tablets every 4 to 6 hours.

Warning: Codeine is a narcotic and may be habit forming. Side effects include drowsiness, respiratory depression, constipation, and nausea. Do not use if allergic to either acetaminophen or codeine.

Muscle Relaxants
Diazepam (Valium®) or Cyclobenzaprine HCL (Flexeril®)

Indications: For the relief of muscle spasms, anxiety, or tension headaches.

Dosage: 5 to 10 mg every 4 to 6 hours.

Warning: This drug will cause drowsiness, fatigue and loss of coordination. It may also slow the victim's rate of breathing, and predispose him to altitude illness. Avoid using above 8,000 feet in altitude.

Migraine Headache
Sumitriptan Succinate injection (Imitrex®)

Indications: For the treatment of migraine or cluster headaches.

Dosage: 6 mg injected subcutaneously using the auto injector.

Warning: Serious cardiac events, including some that have been fatal, have occurred following use of Imitrex® injection. Consult with your physician prior to use. Chest, jaw, or neck tightness is relatively common after administration of Imitrex®.

Altitude Illness
Acetazolamide (Diamox®) 250 mg tablets

Indications: May help to prevent altitude illness when used in conjunction with graded ascent and to treat altitude illness in conjunction with descent. Useful in diminishing the sleep disorder associated with mountain sickness.

Dosage: For prevention, 125 mg (½ tablet) twice a day, beginning the day before the ascent. For treatment, 250 mg twice a day until symptoms resolve.

Warning: Diamox® is not a substitute for graded ascent and acclimatization, nor a substitute for descent in the event of severe altitude illness. Side effects include increased urination, numbness in the fingers and toes, and lethargy. Carbonated beverages will also taste terrible. Do not use if allergic to sulfa medications.

Dexamethasone (Decadron®)

Indications: For the treatment of High Altitude Cerebral Edema (HACE) in conjunction with immediate descent to a lower altitude.

Dosage: 8 mg initially, followed by 4 mg every 6 hours.

Warning: Dexamethasone use can be associated with many side effects. Please consult with your physician before using this medicine.

Nifedipine (Procardia®)

Indications: For the treatment of High Altitude Pulmonary Edema (HAPE) in conjunction with immediate descent to a lower altitude.

Indications: 10 mg every 4 hours or 10 mg one time, followed by 30 mg extended release capsule every 12 to 24 hours.

Warning: May cause low blood pressure and fainting, especially when standing up from a lying position. Do not use if you have any heart disease.

Evacuating an Injured Person

THE DECISION TO EVACUATE AN INJURED or ill member of a party depends on a combination of factors:

- The severity and extent of the victim's injuries or illness
- The distance to medical care or mechanized transportation
- The impact of the evacuation on the safety of the other members of the party
- The medical capability, skills, and resources of the party
- The weather and terrain

Helicopters can be extremely useful for backcountry evacuation, but they may be unavailable or grounded because of bad weather.

Many parties will not have enough individuals to carry a victim very far in the wilderness. It usually requires at least six rescuers to carry a victim in a litter even a short distance (up to 1 mile) over relatively flat terrain. With six rescuers, four can carry the litter while the other two clear the area in the direction of travel and assist in any difficult spots.

If evacuation resources are inadequate, it is best to camp and wait for professional rescue. It would be ill advised, for example, to fabricate a suboptimal litter for transporting a victim with a suspected spine injury over difficult terrain.

If help is to be summoned, it is always best to send two people out whenever possible. The "away team" should be the strongest members of the party, and they should clearly mark or reconnoiter the route so they can lead rescuers back to the victim.

The away team should write down the following information before leaving the victim:

- Name, address, and phone number of the victim, the remaining members of the party, and relatives to be notified
- Where, when, and how the accident occurred
- The nature and extent of the victim's injuries
- Medical care provided to the victim at the scene
- How many people are still at the scene, their condition, and their supplies

- A list of equipment that might be needed
- The party's location and any information about potential helicopter landing zones
- Type of terrain

TRANSPORTING THE VICTIM

If you decide to carry the victim, there are a variety of techniques that can be employed to improvise a litter. Regardless of the system used, some general guidelines should always be considered:

1. Ensure that the victim is safe during transport by securing him within the litter so that he cannot slide around or fall out.
2. Immobilize the victim's entire body in such a way as to allow continued assessment during transport.
3. Provide eye protection for the victim so that he is not struck by branches or twigs during transport.
4. Secure the hands of an unconscious victim inside the litter.
5. Provide padding and insulation for the victim to ensure comfort and warmth.
6. Practice on an uninjured person of about the same size before placing the victim in the litter.
7. Belay the litter on steep terrain.
8. Appoint a single leader, and follow his commands.

 Backcountry Tricks
Improvising a Litter

Nonrigid litters can be improvised from a variety of wilderness equipment, clothing, and natural materials. However, **nonrigid litters do not provide support for the spine and should not be used to transport a victim who may have suffered neck or spinal injury.**

Internal-Frame Backpack Litter. For this litter, the victim must be small and light and be able to sit up without assistance. Cut two holes into the bottom of a large internal-frame backpack. Have the victim slide his legs through the holes and sit in the pack facing front, just as a baby would sit in a baby carrier.

Pole-and-Backpack Litter. Tape or tie ski poles, hiking sticks, or sturdy branches together so that they can support the victim's weight. Slip them across the hipbelts of two side-by-side backpacks, between the rescuer's backs and the packs (fig. 65A). The victim sits on the well-padded poles or branches with his arms over the rescuers' shoulders for support (fig. 65B). This system is only suitable for moderate, open terrain since both rescuers must walk side by side with the victim between them.

Figure 65A-B. Ski pole seat.

Blanket or Tarp Litter. A litter can be improvised from a blanket (a plastic tarp, groundcloth, poncho, or tent fly will also work) and two rigid poles (branches, skis, paddles, etc.). The blanket should be about 4 inches longer than the victim at either end. Open the blanket or tarp and lay one pole lengthwise across the center (fig. 66A). Fold enough of the blanket over the pole so that it is wide enough to accommodate the width of the victim. Place the second pole across the center of the folded blanket (fig. 66B), and fold both free edges over the second pole to the first pole (fig. 66C). The victim's weight will hold the litter together. When using a plastic tarp or groundcloth, a second complete wrap is usually needed to keep the material from slipping.

Once the blanket is in place, lash a crosspiece just above and below the ends of the blanket (fig. 66D). Stretch the blanket as tightly as possible while lashing the crosspieces in place to reduce sagging. Trim the crosspieces as close to the main poles as possible to avoid snagging on brush. Test the litter with a noninjured person to be sure it is sturdy enough to support the victim.

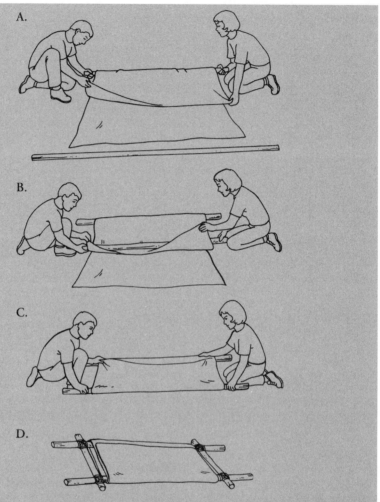

Figure 66A-D. An improvised blanket stretcher.

Spruce, alder, and pine make good stretcher poles. Willow, aspen, and cottonwood are less desirable. They are heavy and flexible when green and are prone to breaking when dead.

Sleeping Bag Litter. Slide two strong branches, ski poles, etc., through either side of a sleeping bag. If necessary, cut two holes in the bottom of the bag so that the poles will slide through. Reinforce the zipper by punching holes through the bag adjacent to the zipper and tying the two halves together with cord. The victim should be placed on top of the bag and not inside.

Parka Litter. Slip two branches, paddles, or skis through the sleeves of two or more heavy parkas (fig. 67). Zip the parkas shut with the sleeves inside to help reinforce the litter. When using skis, tape the edges first to prevent them from tearing through the parkas.

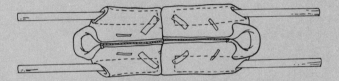

Figure 67. A parka litter.

External-Frame Backpack Frame Litter. A more rigid litter can be constructed from external-frame backpacks. Lash two or more frames together (fig. 68A) and then reinforced with crosspieces (ski poles, paddles, branches). A pack-frame litter can also be constructed by lashing two pack frames to a pair of skis (fig. 68B). The frames should be padded with the victim's sleeping pad.

A.

B.

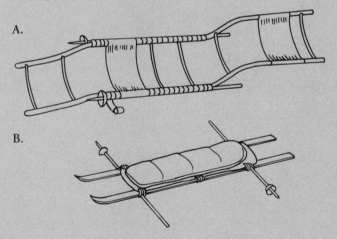

Figure 68. A packframe litter

One-Person Rope-Coil Carry. The split-rope-coil litter uses a coiled climbing rope to allow the rescuer to carry the victim piggyback style. It is good for short-distance transport of a conscious victim, who must be able to support himself and remain upright. Coil the rope on the ground about 2 feet in length and fasten it with a tight wrap. Split the coil into two equal parts (fig. 69A). The victim should place a leg through each part of the split rope (fig. 69B). The rescuer crouches and puts the coils over his shoulders from behind like a pack, and lifts the victim onto his back (fig. 69C). Padding placed between the rope coils and the victim's thighs will dramatically improve the comfort of this system.

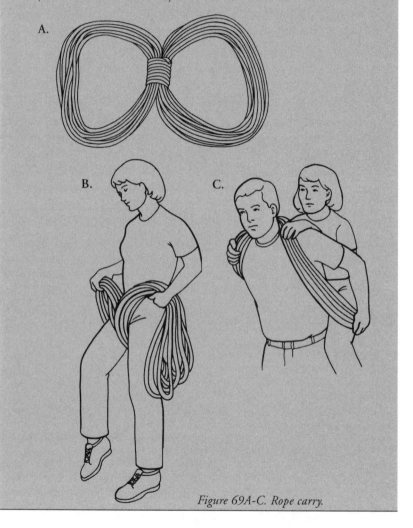

A.

B.

C.

Figure 69A-C. Rope carry.

Index

ABOUT THE AUTHOR

Eric A. Weiss, M.D., F.A.C.E.P., is the Associate Director of Trauma and Emergency Medicine at Stanford University Medical Center and Assistant Professor of Emergency Medicine at Stanford University School of Medicine. He is the founder and medical director of Adventure Medical Kits. He has served as a medical officer for the Himalayan Rescue Association in Nepal and spent three seasons running a medical clinic at 14,000 feet in the Everest region. He provided medical support for a National Geographic Society expedition into the jungles of Belize and was a senior medical officer at the 1996 Summer Olympics.

Prior to and during medical school, Weiss worked as a professional rafting and mountaineering guide. He teaches emergency medicine at the Stanford University School of Medicine and has lectured on wilderness medicine for the past fifteen years throughout the United States and much of the world. The author of *A Comprehensive Guide to Wilderness and Travel Medicine* and *A Field Guide to Wilderness Medicine,* he is a medical consultant to the National Geographic Society, Army Special Forces, and the American Red Cross and currently a member of the board of directors of the Wilderness Medical Society.

The mission of *BACKPACKER* Magazine is to distribute, in a variety of media, credible, in-depth, and compelling "how-to-do-it" information about wilderness recreation, primarily in North America.

BACKPACKER
The Magazine Of Wilderness Travel

BACKPACKER Magazine
33 East Minor Street
Emmaus, PA 18098
website: www.backpacker.com

THE MOUNTAINEERS, founded in 1906, is a nonprofit outdoor activity and conservation club, whose mission is "to explore, study, preserve, and enjoy the natural beauty of the outdoors. . . ." Based in Seattle, Washington, the club is now the third-largest such organization in the United States, with 15,000 members and five branches throughout Washington State.

The Mountaineers sponsors both classes and year-round outdoor activities in the Pacific Northwest, which include hiking, mountain climbing, ski-touring, snowshoeing, bicycling, camping, kayaking and canoeing, nature study, sailing, and adventure travel. The club's conservation division supports environmental causes through educational activities, sponsoring legislation, and presenting informational programs. All club activities are led by skilled, experienced volunteers, who are dedicated to promoting safe and responsible enjoyment and preservation of the outdoors.

If you would like to participate in these organized outdoor activities or the club's programs, consider a membership in The Mountaineers. For information and an application, write or call The Mountaineers, Club Headquarters, 300 Third Avenue West, Seattle, Washington 98119; (206) 284-6310.

The Mountaineers Books, an active, nonprofit publishing program of the club, produces guidebooks, instructional texts, historical works, natural history guides, and works on environmental conservation. All books produced by The Mountaineers are aimed at fulfilling the club's mission.

Send or call for our catalog of more than 300 outdoor titles:

The Mountaineers Books
1001 SW Klickitat Way, Suite 201
Seattle, WA 98134
1-800-553-4453
e-mail: mbooks@mountaineersbooks.org
website: www.mountaineersbooks.org

Other titles you may enjoy from The Mountaineers:

BACKPACKER'S EVERYDAY WISDOM: 1001 Expert Tips for Hikers, Karen Berger
Expert tips and tricks for hikers and backpackers selected from one of the most popular *BACKPACKER* Magazine columns. Covers everything from planning to emergency improvisations.

BACKPACKER'S MAKING CAMP: A Complete Guide for Hikers, Mountain Bikers, Paddlers & Skiers, Steve Howe, Alan Kesselheim, Dennis Coello, John Harlin
A comprehensive, detailed camping how-to compiled by *BACKPACKER* Magazine field experts.

BACKPACKER'S BACKCOUNTRY COOKING: From Pack to Plate in 10 Minutes, Dorcas Miller
More than 144 recipes and trail-tested advice on how to plan and pack simple meals.

BACKPACKER'S LEAVE NO TRACE: A Guide to the New Wilderness Etiquette, Annette McGivney
A comprehensive guide to doable Leave No Trace techniques for all outdoor recreationists. Written by a contributing editor of *BACKPACKER* Magazine.

THE POCKET DOCTOR: Your Ticket to Good Health While Traveling, Third Edition, Stephen Bezruchka, M.D.
A pocket-size guide covering hygiene and health in different environments.

MEDICINE FOR MOUNTAINEERING & OTHER WILDERNESS ACTIVITIES, Fifth Edition, James A. Wilkerson, M.D.
The updated "bible" by climbers/physicians for travelers far from medical help.

ALTITUDE ILLNESS: Prevention & Treatment, Stephen Bezruchka, M.D.
An easy-to-use guide for diagnosing and treating altitude sickness.

HYPOTHERMIA, FROSTBITE, AND OTHER COLD INJURIES: Prevention, Recognition, Prehospital Treatment, James A. Wilkerson, M.D.
A detailed guide covering the signs and symptoms, solutions, and the prevention of cold injuries recommended by the experts.

EMERGENCY SURVIVAL: A Pocket Guide, Christopher Van Tilburg
Indexed information for fast response to medical emergencies—anywhere, anytime.